DANIEL IN BABYLON
STUDY GUIDE

For Individual And Group Study

MICHAEL SCANTLEBURY

Michael Scantlebury has taken author's prerogative in capitalizing certain words that are not usually capitalized according to standard grammatical practice. Also, please note that the name satan and related names are not capitalized as we choose not to acknowledge him, even to the point of disregarding standard grammatical practice.

Study Guide
Daniel In Babylon
ISBN 978-1-7750222-6-8

Legal Deposit – Library and Archives of Canada, 2018

Published by: CreateSpace

Editorial Consultant: Anoja Wijesuriya – 604-265-7320

Cover design by: Michelle Soon – 604-789-9746
Ryele Studio: https://ryele.co/

Books By Michael Scantlebury

Available from Word Alive Press wordalivepress.

DANIEL IN BABYLON
STUDY GUIDE

For Individual And Group Study

MICHAEL SCANTLEBURY

TABLE OF CONTENTS

INTRODUCTION

WELCOME TO . . .

. . . an exciting study into the present truth lifestyle illustrated through the lives of Daniel and his friends. Whether you'll be meeting with others in a group or going through this book on your own, you've made an excellent decision by choosing to read **DANIEL in Babylon** and studying it in-depth with this guide.

HOW TO USE THIS WORKBOOK?

For Individual Use — Any person can benefit from personal study of the Bible passages, quotes, and teachings in this book. Just set aside a few minutes each day to be alone and in silence with the Lord. Ask Him to show you what you need to be learning about His Kingdom — and your personal role within it. List your answers and responses in the blank spaces provided. Be ready to share them with others, too, if you'll be meeting with a small group. Most importantly, try to put some of your insights into practical action.

For use in Small Groups — These sessions work great in a group of 3 to 10 people. Make sure everyone has a book and rotate leaders each week. Participants should try to come to the session having already read the chapter to be discussed.

- **Focusing In**. Here's a short, punchy quotation from Apostle Michael Scantlebury to focus attention on the theme of the study. It's followed by a reflection question and a response question.

- **Responding to the Author/From the Book.** This section is the heart of the study. It contains three or four key quotations from the book DANIEL IN BABYLON. You'll recall what you read and respond with your own insights, applications, and personal evaluation exercises.

- **Applying Your Insights.** Here's a general recap to use each week. You'll have a chance to apply what you've learned and to pray prayers of intercession and thanksgiving as a result.

- **Reviewing in the Word.** This section offers the scriptural references from the chapter topic, which you can use as supplemental readings during the week.

- **For Group Discussion.** These questions form the main portion of your small group study time. You'll draw upon your individual workbook responses to help you answer and interact with others around the topic themes.

- **Closing Prayer.** Make prayer an important part of your group! You might even consider keeping an ongoing record of your prayer requests during the course. Each week you can then review where you have been in prayer. Consider what you have asked and what answers have been provided.

God bless you as you begin this study. Ask the Holy Spirit to open your heart to all that He would have you learn.

— Apostle Michael Scantlebury

CHAPTER 1
BRIEF HISTORY OF ANCIENT BABYLON

Focusing In:

The historical city Babylon has long been destroyed but the spirit of Babylon has remained and is well entrenched in the earth today. Revelation Chapters 17-18 gives us some significant understanding into this spirit of Babylon.

However, as we broach this study it would be beneficial if we were to take a journey back into the history of this nation.

— Apostle Michael Scantlebury

Reflect:

The word Babylon is Akkadian "babilani" which means "the gate of god(s)" and it became the capital of the land of Babylonia. The etymology of the name Babel in the Bible means "confused" (Genesis 11:9) and throughout the Bible, Babylon was a symbol of the confusion caused by godlessness. Is it possible, that we, to-date are engulfed in this confusion that was created several centuries ago? According to the word of God, what was the root cause for this state of confusion? Do we have to continue to live in this state of confusion?

Respond:

Genesis 11:1-9 describes the building of the city and its famous tower "whose top may reach unto heaven." It also records how and why God came down and punished the people's arrogance by creating a confusion of different languages and possibly their racial distinctions.

Throughout the long period of Babylonian history, the Babylonians achieved a high level of civilization that made an impact on the whole known world.

One of the main aspects of Babylonian culture was a codified system of law.

Now let's take our journey into the life of Daniel in Babylon and draw some truths that we could live by in today's world.

RESPONDING TO THE AUTHOR

In Chapter 1 of DANIEL in Babylon, Apostle Michael Scantlebury makes the statements below. Think about each one for a moment, and then respond to the questions/exercises in the spaces provided.

From the Book: *Ancient Babylon.*

The tremendous wealth and power of this city, along with its monumental size and appearance, were certainly considered a Biblical myth, that is, until its foundations were unearthed and its riches substantiated during the 19th century. Archaeologists stood in awe as their discoveries revealed that certain stories in the Bible were actual situations that had happened in time.

- The City of Babylon was the _____ of _____ in _____ Mesopotamia?

1. Where was this situated from a modern-day perception? ____

_____

_____

_____

_____

2. What is the meaning of the word Babylon? What are its roots?

_____

_____

_____

_____

_____

From the Book: *The Location of Babylon*

Babylon lies in the land of Shinar as revealed in the Bible (Genesis10:10) and its general location has never been disputed. Babylonia was situated in the area known as Mesopotamia (Greek for "between the rivers").

3. Who occupies this geographical location today? _____

_____

_____

_____

_____

_____

4. What are the _____ great rivers that flowed through this land?
   Where does their course run from? _____

_____

_____

_____

_____

_____

- Along these two rivers were many great trading cities such as
  _____ and _____ on the Euphrates.

- _____ rests on a _____ with the
  two large rivers flowing through it, the _____ and
  _____. Their course runs from _____ and
  _____ to the _____ _____. Mountains
  surround the _____ and _____ sides of the plain, the
  _____ chain and _____, and the _____ and
  _____ deserts guard the west and south.

From the Book: *The Tower of Babel.*

The Bible reveals that all false systems of religion began in the land of Babylon. It is interesting to note that every organized system of religion in the world today has traces of ancient Babylon. The Bible records in Genesis 10:10 that, after the great flood, all men spoke one common language and a man named Nimrod built a city and established a common religion. Nimrod was a descendant of Noah's son, Ham.

5. What lead to the common language spoken by the people being
   confused? _____

_____

_____

_____

_____

_____

6. What does Genesis 11:4 has to say about this? _____

_____

_____

_____

_____

7. Do you believe that Nimrod was the one to be blamed for creating complete chaos in the then Babylon, continuing to date? Why? _____

_____

_____

_____

_____

▪ This way man would be forced to _____ God's original command to "be fruitful and fill the whole earth." It is interesting that the _____ used to build the Tower of Babel were the same as those employed for the construction of the great _____ of Babylon and similar ziggurats, according to ancient building inscriptions.

- There is evidence that man has lived in this area of _____ since the beginning of civilization. The first records indicate that _____ was established as a city around the _____. Before this it was a _____ capital ruled by the _____of the city of ____. Then came the migration of the _____.

From the Book: *Overview of Babylonian History*

Babylonia (pronounced babilahnia) was an ancient empire that existed in the Near East in southern Mesopotamia. Throughout much of their history their main rival for supremacy, were their neighbours, the Assyrians. It was the Babylonians, under King Nebuchadnezzar II, who destroyed Jerusalem, the capital of the kingdom of Judah, and carried God's covenant people into captivity in 587 BC.

8. Around 2000 BC Hammurapi emerged as the ruler of Babylonia. What were the significant changes that he brought about in the land? _____

_____

_____

_____

_____

9. What other significant act took place around this same time in the city of Ur? _____

_____

_____

_____

_____

_____

10. Under whose leadership did Babylonia finally win its independence? Which time period was this? _____

_____

_____

_____

_____

_____

11. What became of Babylon under King Nebuchadnezzar II the son of Nabopolassar? _____

_____

_____

_____

_____

_____

12. As foretold by prophet Jeremiah, the Israelites were to return to Jerusalem after_____years of their captivity, which occurred in 587 BC. During this time, the Lord encouraged His

people though_____and _____who were also captives in Babylon. What significant occurrence took place by the end of this time period? _____

_____

_____

_____

_____

_____

12. By the end of Babylonian rule spanning a 70 years, they were able to achieve a high level of civilization culminating their religious beliefs and the codified system of law, which impacted the whole known world. How will you describe the Babylonian religion? _____

_____

_____

_____

_____

_____

13. What are the _____Babylonian cities that are mentioned in Genesis 10:10 and who ruled these cities along with the Assyria? _____

_____

_____

_____

_____

_____

14. Who was the modern day leader who is reported to have spent billions of dollars in recreating the hanging gardens of Babylon? _____

_____

_____

_____

_____

15. Where in the Bible can we find the, well entrenched, spirit of Babylon being described?_____

_____

_____

_____

_____

16. What can we conclude from the accounts in Revelation 17:1-6; 18:1-4 _____

_____

_____

_____

_____

_____

APPLYING YOUR INSIGHTS

1. Review what you've written and learned in this workbook chapter. As further thoughts or ideas come to mind, list them below. (Include questions or comments that you would like to raise when your small group meets.) _____

_____

_____

_____

_____

2. What was the most meaningful concept or truth in this chapter of Daniel in Babylon – A Brief History of Ancient Babylon? How will this enrich your life, of family, church, or community? _____

_____

_____

_____

_____

3. Take some time to pray and intercede — for yourself, your family, your church, your city, and the world. List some of your most pressing needs and requests here: _____

_____

_____

_____

_____

_____

4. Take some time to pray and give thanks. What blessing and joys has God brought into your life this week? Name some of them here? _____

_____

_____

_____

_____

_____

REVIEWING IN THE WORD

Be sure to check out these Scriptures related to the topic of "Brief History of Ancient Babylon"

Genesis 11:1-9   Revelation 18:1-4

Genesis 10:10   Revelation 17:1-6

FOR GROUP DISCUSSION

In your small group, discuss one or more of the following, as time permits

1. Use your opening moments to share some of your major insights, comments, or questions from your reading of Chapter 1, Brief History of Ancient Babylon. (Refer to your individual Workbook responses, as well.)

2. Apostle Michael Scantlebury says, "The historical city Babylon has long been destroyed but the spirit of Babylon has remained and is well entrenched in the earth today." How does this statement strike you?

3. What is meant by "the spirit of Babylon"? Have you seen/experienced this spirit operating in any of your leaders? In yourself?

4. Read aloud Revelation chapters 17 and 18. Discuss the nature of this spirit and how it operates in our midst even to-date?

5. Can you explain in brief "So then, Babylon could be better described as a system, which is socioeconomic, political and religious; existing today!"

****

Close your group time in prayer ......

CHAPTER 2

DANIEL'S ENTRY INTO BABYLON

Focusing In:

Judah was not completely destroyed, but was looted extensively. This invasion is referred to as the first deportation. King Nebuchadnezzar conquered Judah, took all the vessels from the Temple and deported the healthiest of the Hebrews back to Babylonia to be slaves. Judah was made a vassal state and was allowed to keep its king. Daniel was among those taken into captivity.

— Apostle Michael Scantlebury

Reflect:

The ten northern tribes called Israel had been taken into captivity approximately 722 B.C. This left only the two southern tribes called Judah in the land of Israel. Judah also was taken into captivity beginning first with an invasion by the Chaldean king, King Nebuchadnezzar. Why would God allow His own people who were called by His name to be invaded and ransacked in this manner?

Respond:

Jeremiah 25:1-11 and 2 Chronicles 36:14-21 explains the reasons God allowed these invasions to take place.

According to these Scriptures, God's stated reasons for allowing the destruction of Judah and their deportation were:

- They continued with their idolatry.

- They mocked and abused God's messengers.

- They failed to give the land the sabbatical years.

RESPONDING TO THE AUTHOR

In Chapter 2 of DANIEL in Babylon, Apostle Michael Scantlebury makes the statements below. Think about each one for a moment, and then respond to the questions/exercises in the spaces provided.

From the Book: *Israel's Failures – Idolatry*

Idolatry is worshiping any created thing. God's First Commandment is "to have no other Gods before Me." (Exodus 20:3) Israel came into being at the divine decree of God. He made them a peculiar people, to whom He would give the special privilege of revealing Himself to the world.

1. How do you think God wanted Israel to represent Him to the rest of the nations? Do you believe there was a responsibility attached to the privilege that they were given by God? _____

_____

_____

_____

_____

2. What are some of the special promises that He gave to the Children of Israel? _____

_____

_____

_____

_____

_____

3. They chose to worship inanimate objects such as stones, trees, rivers and a host of other things in nature. They worshipped the heavenly bodies as the sun, moon and stars, instead of obeying God. What can be the reason for such behaviour as this? Are we today imitating this same behavior? _____

_____

_____

_____

_____

4. God's love is shown in that even when man willingly rejected Him, He would not be deterred from His plan to save man. Where in the bible does God talk about the continuity of this plan? _____

_____

_____

_____

_____

From the Book: *Israel's Failures – They despised the Word of God, mocking and misusing God's messengers.*

It should be understood that not all of the Hebrews rejected God. Through Israel's history there were those few who believed God and longed for the day when their nation and its leaders would also.

These Believers were always the minority and were always oppressed and persecuted by those who practiced false religion. These true Saints and Prophets believed and taught God's truth, which offended the hypocrites and leaders of false religion within their nation. These wicked men hated the very word of God because it exposed their false teachings and their sins. Their shameful treatment of God's messengers the Prophets, is clear evidence of their despising the Word of God. The messenger was the one who delivered the Word of God, but the message was from God! Yet, with no apparent fear of God, they imprisoned and murdered many of the Prophets God sent to them.

5. There were _____ who had not bowed down to idols among the Israelites? How would you describe these people? _____

_____

_____

_____

_____

6. What similarities do you observe between those people and us, the modern day Believer? _____

_____

_____

_____

_____

_____

7. What does Hebrews 11:36-40 have to say about the people who at that point in time chose to continue to walk in righteousness? Does this have any relevance to us today? _____

_____

_____

_____

_____

From the Book: _Israel's Failures_

They refused to observe the Sabbatical years. In Leviticus 25:1-7, God directed the Children of Israel to allow the land to rest each seventh year. After the forty-ninth year they were to declare a special "jubilee" in which all land returned to its original owner and slaves were returned to their families.

8. What did God promise to Israel every sixth year; and where in the Bible do we find reference to this promise? _____

_____

_____

_____

_____

Why did God want the Israelites to give this Sabbatical rest to the land? Was there a spiritual principle that He wanted His people to understand? _____

_____

_____

_____

_____

_____

9. As 2 Chronicles 36:21 states the land rested for seventy years. How and when did this come about? _____

_____

_____

_____

_____

_____

10. What could have spared Israel from this judgement of being sent into captivity? _____

_____

_____

_____

_____

_____

11. What was God really testing in His people by asking them to give this Sabbatical rest to the land? How does this parallel to Abraham? _____

_____

_____

_____

_____

_____

From the Book: *The background on the book of Daniel*

"The modern Bible places the Book of Daniel as the first of the Minor Prophets, as well as did the LXX (The Septuagint [70], the Greek translation of the Hebrew Old testament) and the Vulgate (Latin Bible). However, in the Hebrew Bible the Book of Daniel is placed among the Poetic Books of Psalms, Proverbs, Job, Song of Solomon, Ruth, Lamentations, Ecclesiastes, Ester, Daniel, Ezra, Nehemiah, 1st and 2nd Chronicles.

We know nothing of the early life of Daniel, except what is recorded in the Book bearing his name. Here it is said that he was one of the youths of royal or noble seed, who were carried captive by Nebuchadnezzar in the third year of Jehoiakim, king of Judah."

12. Why is it that Daniel cannot be considered a Prophet in the normal sense? _____

_____

_____

_____

_____

_____

13. What then, is the reason for considering Daniel a Prophet?

_____

_____

_____

_____

_____

14. What were the objections brought forth the liberal unbelieving scholars to reject Daniel as the author of this book? _____

_____

_____

_____

_____

15. How then can we be sure that Daniel was the author of this book?

_____

_____

From the Book: *About the Prophet Daniel*

"Daniel's name means, "God is Judge". In Ezekiel 14:14, 20, the righteousness of Daniel is attested to as well as to his wisdom in Ezekiel 28:3"

16. What has the bible to say about Daniel's decent? Which Scriptures talks about his lineage? _____

----

17. What are the events leading to Daniel and the Hebrew boys being taken into captivity? _____

----

18. What was known as the Carchemish fortress of Chemosh? And what was its geographical location? What was the significance of this place? _____

_____

_____

_____

_____

19. What did King Nebuchadnezzar place in the temple of his idol god Bel-Marduk after the siege of Jerusalem in 587 BC? _____

_____

_____

_____

_____

20. Do you believe there are lessons/insights we could use in the 21st Century from that which is recorded of the happenings back then? Why? _____

_____

_____

_____

APPLYING YOUR INSIGHTS

Review what you've written and learned in this workbook chapter. As further thoughts or ideas come to mind, list them below. (Include questions or comments that you would like to raise when your small group meets.)

1. What was the most meaningful concept or truth in this chapter of Daniel In Babylon – Daniel's Entry into Babylon? How will this enrich your life of family, church, or community? _____

_____

_____

_____

_____

2. Take some time to pray and intercede — for yourself, your family, your church, your city, and the world. List some of your most pressing needs and requests here: _____

_____

_____

_____

_____

3. Take some time to pray and give thanks. What blessing and joys has God brought into your life this week? Name some of them here? _____

_____

_____

_____

_____

_____

REVIEWING IN THE WORD

Be sure to check out these Scriptures related to the topic of "Daniel's Entry into Babylon"

Jeremiah 25:1-11	Exodus 20:3
2 Chronicles 36:14-21	1 Kings 19:18
Leviticus 25:1-7	Leviticus 25:21-22
Leviticus 25:1-27	2 Chronicles 36:3-4
Daniel 9:2	Daniel 12:4
Daniel 1:3, 6	1 Chronicles 3:1
Ezra 1:1	Ezekiel 14:14, 20
Ezekiel 28:3	Jeremiah 22:19
Jeremiah 25:1	2 Kings 23:33-35
2 Kings 24:1	2 Kings 24:6
Matthew 24:15	Mark 13:14
John 16:2	Acts 1:15-26

Romans 5:8   Romans 1:21-23

Hebrews 11:36-40

FOR GROUP DISCUSSION

In your small group, discuss one or more of the following, as time permits!

1. Use your opening moments to share some of your major insights, comments, or questions from your reading of Chapter 2, Daniel's Entry into Babylon. (Refer to your individual Workbook responses, as well.)

2. Apostle Michael Scantlebury says, "God wanted Israel to live by faith and live according to His promises, yet they would not. They refused to trust God to meet their needs." What are your thoughts on this statement?

3. What is meant by the word "Apocalyptic"? Have you seen/experienced this outpouring in any of your leaders? In yourself?

4. Read aloud 2 Chronicles 36:14-21. Discuss as to how this Scripture applies to us today.

5. Apostle Michael Scantlebury talks about a set of Hebrews who did not reject God and these believers always being a minority. What does this mean and how does it impact you?

6. Discuss what God's stated reasons are for allowing the destruction of Judah and their deportation? Are we today far from committing similar atrocities and therefore not liable for punishment?

7. Why is the book of Daniel referred to as the Book of Revelation of the Old Testament? How does it impact us today?

8. What were the reasons for God's messengers to be hated and ill-treated? Do we see similar behavioural patterns in this day and age?

****

Close your group time in prayer ......

CHAPTER 3

APOSTLES IN TRAINING

Focusing In:

I believe that Daniel and his friends were Apostles, as they were "sent" by God into Babylon, rather than the Babylonians capturing and incarcerating them.

Remember that the word "Apostle" comes from the Greek verb *apostello*, which in its simplest form means "*sent one*".

— Apostle Michael Scantlebury

Reflect:

We would like to view Daniel and his colleagues to represent the "Present Day Apostolic Church", or as Strong, Spirit-Filled Believers living in this present world system and being able to stand strong upon biblical principles. They represent a lethal mentality that would not bow to satanic pressure. Did God really allow His own messenger to be taken to a different land under captivity? Can we be also sent into the same or similar circumstances? Do we recognize these instances in our lives and act accordingly… just like Daniel and his friends did?

Respond:

In Chapter 1 of Daniel we read the account about how King Nebuchadnezzar of Babylon, besieged Jerusalem and destroyed it and took the best and the brightest to influence and strengthen his domain. His kingdom was very expansive; it covered most of the then middle east.

This is still happening today, the devil and his agents are forever making forays into the Church seeking the best and the brightest to expand his kingdom.

RESPONDING TO THE AUTHOR

In Chapter 3 of DANIEL in Babylon, Apostle Michael Scantlebury makes the statements below. Think about each one for a moment, and then respond to the questions/exercises in the spaces provided.

From the Book: *Daniel Was a Real Man in the Real World*

We are called to live in this world but not be a part of its system. We have to live right in the corruption; however, we must live with style and an overcoming nature. There are several things that are recorded in the Book of Daniel that gives us great insight as to how the enemy works in seeking to capture and desensitize Christians from the truth of God's Word and the leading of His Holy Spirit.

1. As modern day Believers, what are the 3 most crucial things that we are not called to do? _____

_____

_____

_____

_____

_____

2. What can we learn from the first five versus of Daniel Chapter 1 in terms of Training? How does this translate to us as Christians living in the World System "a type of Babylon"?

_____

_____

_____

_____

_____

3. According to Daniel 1:3-8 what is the Key to functioning in this World System? _____

_____

_____

_____

_____

_____

4. Daniel was taken along with his _____ friends and they were _____ in Babylon. They were between the ages of _____ years and the 12 Chapters of the Book of Daniel span over a _____ year period. So then, Daniel's life presents a very successful life in the world system. After all he stood strong as an influential figure under _____ successive kings and _____ successive kingdoms, of Babylon and Medo-Persia and he remained _____ the whole time. This leads us to understand that God is always relevant; it is the people's _____ of Him that is not. He is the Alpha and the Omega (the beginning and the end). He can fit right into any

generation, circumstance or situation. He is _____!

5. According to the recorded word, what are some of the schemes the enemy used in seeking to capture and desensitize these Hebrew boys?

6. Can it be possible that we as Christians living in a type of "Babylon" be exposed to similar tactics from the enemy? How are we to navigate through such adversity?

From the Book: *The Issue of Training*

The word training is derived from a very interesting Hebrew word; it is the word gadal: to become strong, to be powerful, to become valuable. It identifies a continuous, developmental process of growth towards greatness. In this context, it was to be used in the service of Babylon.

7. What is the need of the hour for the Church of Jesus Christ on earth now at a time when unlike Daniel and his friends, the young talented individuals have not been able to withstand the aggressive training and schooling? _____

8. What has caused the Church to be ineffective in advancing The Kingdom in us? _____

_____

_____

_____

_____

_____

9. What is the Mandate from Jesus to the early Apostles and by extension to us? _____

_____

_____

_____

_____

10. How different is the response of these early Believers from us today? _____

_____

_____

_____

_____

11. Where did the devil steal the principle of training? _____

_____

_____

_____

_____

_____

12. What are the 4 major factors to be considered in executing a successful Kingdom Training Principle? _____

_____

_____

_____

_____

_____

13. How will you surmise what Babylon is? _____

_____

_____

_____

_____

APPLYING YOUR INSIGHTS

1. Review what you've written and learned in this workbook chapter. As further thoughts or ideas come to mind, list them below. (Include questions or comments that you would like to

raise when your small group meets.) _____

_____

_____

_____

_____

_____

2. What was the most meaningful concept or truth in this chapter of Daniel In Babylon – Apostles in Training? How will this enrich your life of family, church, or community? ____

_____

_____

_____

_____

_____

3. Take some time to pray and intercede — for yourself, your family, your church, your city, and the world. List some of your most pressing needs and requests here: _____

_____

_____

_____

_____

_____

4. Take some time to pray and give thanks. What blessing and joys has God brought into your life this week? Name some of them here? _____

_____

_____

_____

_____

_____

REVIEWING IN THE WORD

Be sure to check out these Scriptures related to the topic of "Apostles in Training"

Daniel 1:3-5, 8   Matthew 28:18-20

Romans 1:21-23   Philippians 3:12-14

1 Timothy 4:12-16   2 Timothy 3:14-17

FOR GROUP DISCUSSION

In your small group, discuss one or more of the following, as time permits:

1. Use your opening moments to share some of your major insights, comments, or questions from your reading of Chapter 3, Apostles In Training. (Refer to your individual Workbook responses, as well.)

2. Apostle Michael Scantlebury says, "We cannot afford to live our lives with the idea that the world is coming to an end tomorrow and as such we do not make any plans for ourselves

and that of our offspring." What are your thoughts on this statement?

3. What is meant by the word "gadal"? Have you experienced this in your own life or in the lives of your loved ones the magnitude of chaos caused by the evil one using this powerful biblical principle? Do you believe there is a great untapped opportunity available for us to use this for our advantage, and sending out into the World, Christians who are trained and engrained in the principles of the Kingdom just like Daniel and his friends?

4. Read aloud 2 Timothy 3:14-17. Discuss as to how this Scripture applies to us today.

5. Apostle Michael Scantlebury talks about Babylon being described as anything or any set of circumstances that is organized to rob the Kingdom Reality from our lives. What does this mean and how does it impact you?

6. Discuss why it is important for us to have a Futuristic Mentality on Life?

7. Jesus spoke to twelve Disciples, most of them unlearned (according to Babylonian Standards) and instructed them to go into the world and preach the good news and they believed Him, stepped out and accomplished it. In your perspective what prevents us today from being able to have a global focus in expanding His Kingdom on Earth?

8. "Training" being a biblical principle that the devil has stolen from the Kingdom of God, What practical steps can we take in re-claiming and using it for the advancing of the Kingdom of God on earth?

****

Close your group time in prayer ......

CHAPTER 4
THE ISSUE OF
IDENTITY

Focusing In:

The first thing that I would like for us to notice is who Babylon went after: "…young men in whom there were no blemishes, but good-looking, gifted in all wisdom, possessing knowledge and quick to understand, who had ability to serve in the king's palace, and whom they might teach the language and literature…"

— Apostle Michael Scantlebury

Reflect:

Remember that we are looking at Babylon as a type of the world system and Daniel and his friends as any modern day, Spirit-filled, committed Believer. In light of this I believe that several of you reading this book would have qualified to be either Daniel or one of the three young men that were incarcerated in Babylon. Who is it that the world system is still after?

Respond: Daniel 1:1-7

"Then the king instructed Ashpenaz, the master of his eunuchs, to bring some of the children of Israel and some of the king's descendants and some of the nobles, 4 young men in whom there was no blemish, but good-looking, gifted in all wisdom, possessing knowledge and quick to understand, who had ability to serve in the king's palace, and whom they might teach the language and literature of the Chaldeans."

According to the Scripture above Babylon (the world's system) is still after:

- Those in whom there is no blemish (righteous).

- Those who are good-looking (the Image of Jesus Christ).

- Those who are gifted in all wisdom (Wisdom of God).

- Those possessing knowledge (the One that comes from above).

- Those who are quick to understand (Spirit-Filled).

- Those who have the ability to serve in the king's palace (already serving the True King; Jesus Christ).

These are the ones Babylon wants to attract in-order to be trained, as they already possess a solid and strong foundation in God.

RESPONDING TO THE AUTHOR

In Chapter 4 of DANIEL in Babylon, Apostle Michael Scantlebury makes the statements below. Think about each one for a moment, and then respond to the questions/exercises in the spaces provided.

From the Book: *Identity and Function*

Not only does Babylon want to "train" you, but they also want to change your identity and function. I find it very interesting that for most when referring to Daniel and the three Hebrew boys that were incarcerated in Babylon, they are referred to as Shadrach, Meshach and Abednego.

1. During Bible times the name given to a child stood for much and had a _____ about it that the names of individuals no longer carry.

2. Contrast the meanings of the names of the four Hebrew boys and the meanings of the names that Babylon inflicted upon them:

Hebrew Name	Name inflicted by Babylon
- Daniel:	- Belteshazzar:
- Hananiah:	- Shadrach:
- Mishael:	- Meshach:
- Azariah:	- Abednego:

3. Why would Babylon want to change our names? Why is our identity in God so important to Babylon? _____

_____

_____

_____

_____

_____

APPLYING YOUR INSIGHTS

1. Review what you've written and learned in this workbook chapter. As further thoughts or ideas come to mind, list them below. (Include questions or comments that you would like to raise when your small group meets.) _____

_____

_____

_____

_____

2. What was the most meaningful concept or truth in this chapter of Daniel in Babylon – The Issue of Identity? How will this enrich your life, of family, church, or community? ___

_____

_____

_____

_____

3. Take some time to pray and intercede — for yourself, your family, your church, your city, and the world. List some of your most pressing needs and requests here: _____

_____

_____

_____

_____

4. Take some time to pray and give thanks. What blessing and joys has God brought into your life this week? Name some of them here? _____

_____

_____

REVIEWING IN THE WORD

Be sure to check out these Scriptures related to the topic of "The Issue of Identity"

Daniel 1:1-7   Deuteronomy 7:1-11   Deuteronomy 18:9-14

FOR GROUP DISCUSSION

In your small group, discuss one or more of the following, as time permits.

1. Use your opening moments to share some of your major insights, comments, or questions from your reading of Chapter 4, The Issue of Identity. (Refer to your individual Workbook responses, as well.)

2. Apostle Michael Scantlebury says, "The Kingdom of God and the Church of Jesus Christ have been called out of the world and must live as through we have been." How does this statement strike you?

3. The words that God spoke to the Children of Israel before they entered the promise land in Deuteronomy 7:1-11. … Is it relevant to us today?

4. What is the kind of training that we are offered on this world system? Can we benefit from this training and under what circumstances?

4. Have you or any one you are affiliated to have benefited from such training?

5. In spite of all effort by the world system have you been able to hold on to your identity? Describe how?

****

Close your group time in prayer ......

CHAPTER 5

IDENTITY OF THE NEW TESTAMENT CHURCH

Focusing In:

The New Testament Church is called out of the world to become God's own, special people! 1 Peter 2:8-9

The New Testament Church is also given a separate identity as recorded by Apostle Paul in Philippians 2:5-15.

— Apostle Michael Scantlebury

Reflect:

It is incredibly significant and interesting that the Lord will call His Church, the Ecclesia. Interestingly, it was in the book of Daniel that God first revealed the fact that His Kingdom will be coming into the Earth. In much the same way we see the first direct mention and understanding of The Kingdom of God came at the time when the most powerful kingdom (Babylon) existed, in like manner we are hearing about the Ecclesia/Church at a time when the most organized and intelligent kingdom (Roman Expire) existed.

Respond:

Matthew 16:18 - Jesus Christ first used the word Church to introduce a whole new dynamic to His early Apostles. That word Church is translated from the Greek ecclesia meaning assembly. As a matter of fact, the Roman Senate was also an ecclesia or assembly.

The Roman Empire was a kingdom; it was not a democracy like many of today's governments and contrary to popular opinion it was closer to what The Kingdom of God looked like.

That is why Jesus could have spoken about kingdom with such relevance to a point that some thought He came to set up a rival kingdom to Rome and to b in direct opposition to Caesar.

RESPONDING TO THE AUTHOR

In Chapter 5 of DANIEL in Babylon, Apostle Michael Scantlebury makes the statements below. Think about each one for a moment, and then respond to the questions/exercises in the spaces provided.

From the Book: The Church

When Jesus Christ first used the word *Church* in Matthew Chapter 16 it was to introduce a whole new dynamic to His early Apostles. That word Church comes from the Greek *ecclesia (Ekklesia)* meaning assembly. As a matter of fact, the Roman Senate was also an ecclesia or assembly.

1. What are the root words and their meanings, which contribute towards forming the word Ekklesia? _____

_____

_____

_____

_____

2. What is the deeper meaning of this word "Ekklesia"? _____

_____

_____

_____

_____

3. Where did the word Ecclesia (Ekklesia) originate? For what purpose? _____

_____

_____

_____

_____

4. What is the parallel between Caesars senate and us as Christians? _____

_____

_____

_____

_____

From the Book: _Acquiring New Territory_

One of the most amazing truths is how the Roman Government would acquire new territory — here's what they did.

Rome would seize a nation by using the strategies of its Senate (Eccelesia) whereby Roman businessmen would set up businesses in the heart of a city and once firmly entrenched into that society, the armies of Rome would seize power over the city and it succumbed to Roman rule. These Roman businessmen lived in the city, but were not of the city.

5. How does this contrast with what Jesus Christ intended for the Church... His Ecclesia?_____

_____

_____

_____

_____

_____

6. What was the Church never intended to be? _____

_____

_____

_____

_____

7. What is it that Jesus Christ wants to accomplish on earth through the Church? _____

_____

_____

_____

_____

8. What is the sure promise that Jesus gave the True Church in His bold declaration to Apostle Peter? _____

_____

_____

_____

_____

9. The true _____ will be the possessor of the _____ of The Kingdom of God. Ergo, accurate access to _____ is through His Church. The Church must be built upon the _____ that comes from the Father and not through _____ and _____, i.e. traditions, festivals, holy days, works, etc.

From the Book: *Our Destiny*

Philippians 2:15 — speaks to our Identity as the people of God in the earth. As a matter of fact I like to call this our *destination* verse. Strong people who know their Identity! However, to arrive at verse 15 the foundation is laid in verse 5. It begins with a certain type of mentality!

10. What are the elements of the type of mindset that we as Christians are to possess? _____

_____

_____

_____

11. Is there any real danger from this world system, in us operating under this mindset? Can you think of an example from your own life? _____

_____

_____

_____

_____

12. Detail some of the principles that we can glean from Daniel and his friends in terms of not dropping the standards and compromising our very identity as members of the ecclesia?

_____

_____

_____

_____

13. How did God respond to Daniel and his friends who purposed in their heart not to compromise, lose their identity?

_____

_____

_____

_____

_____

_____

14. What significance does this have for us today? _____

_____

_____

_____

_____

- Apostle Paul by the _____of the Holy Spirit gave us the _____
  ___ for living a successful Christian life while functioning in
  the midst of a _____ and _____ gene-ration.
  He to us how to be _____ in   the
  midst of the world's darkness. He shared with us that we
  would need to _____ our salvation.

From the Book: _Salvation is a lifestyle_

Work out your own Salvation: initial Salvation (being Born-Again)
is only the entry point. Then it is a constant work- in essence it is
to do something from which there is a result. Unlike religion, that
allows you to do, things from which there is no result.

15. What is the purpose for Apostle Paul to encourage us to per-form
    until something productive happens all the while making sure that
    we do not complain or dispute? Philippians 2:14

_____

_____

_____

_____

_____

16. Do you believe that establishing our identity is an individual thing? Support your response with an example from the Bible of a personal transformation before coming into the fullness of what God wanted to do through this individual's life? _____

_____

_____

_____

_____

_____

17. Are you confident that you are like Daniel and his friends in terms of making a firm commitment not to allow this world system to change your identity? _____

_____

_____

_____

_____

_____

18. Do you know of friends and family who have allowed this world system to distort their identity? What can be done to help these individuals regain their lost identity and ensure that

our young ones remain steadfast and committed to maintaining their identity? _____

_____

_____

_____

_____

- What we are doing is _____ the _____ for the operations in Daniel's life. We are viewing Daniel's life and that of his friends and _____ operational ___ _____ as a 21st Century Church.

APPLYING YOUR INSIGHTS

1. Review what you've written and learned in this workbook chapter. As further thoughts or ideas come to mind, list them below. (Include questions or comments that you would like to raise when your small group meets.) _____

_____

_____

_____

_____

2. What was the most meaningful concept or truth in this chapter

of Daniel in Babylon – Identity of the New Testament Church? How will this enrich your life, of family, church, or community? _____

_____

_____

_____

_____

_____

3. Take some time to pray and intercede — for yourself, your family, your church, your city, and the world. List some of your most pressing needs and requests here: _____

_____

_____

_____

_____

_____

4. Take some time to pray and give thanks. What blessing and joys has God brought into your life this week? Name some of them here? _____

_____

_____

_____

REVIEWING IN THE WORD

Be sure to check out these Scriptures related to the topic of "Identity of the New Testament Church"

Genesis 32:22-31   Daniel 1:17

Matthew 13:18-23   Matthew 16:

Philippians 2:5-15   1 Peter 2:8-9

FOR GROUP DISCUSSION

In your small group, discuss one or more of the following, as time permits

1. Use your opening moments to share some of your major insights, comments, or questions from your reading of Chapter 5, Identity of the New Testament Church. (Refer to your individual Workbook responses, as well.)

2. Apostle Michael Scantlebury says, "Every false religion and cult in the earth has a process of learning and training and desire, except the true Church of Jesus Christ, but that is changing. We need to be involved in increasing and learning." What are your thoughts on this statement?

3. What is meant by the word "Ecclesia"? Have you seen/experienced this understanding in carrying out the daily operations among your leaders? In yourself?

4. Read aloud Matthew chapter 13 versus 18 to 23 and discuss as to how it applies to our lives.

5. Can you explain in brief what you understand by "We must stand reject this present world order. We must stand in the power and identity of Jesus Christ."

****

Close your group time in prayer ......

CHAPTER 6

THE ISSUE OF VEGETABLES

Focusing In: *Proverbs 23:1-3*

> "When you sit down to eat with a ruler, consider carefully what is before you; [2] and put a knife to your throat if you are a man given to appetite. [3] Do not desire his delicacies, for they are deceptive food."

— Apostle Michael Scantlebury

Reflect:

As these young men were incarcerated in Babylon, one of the first orders of business for the Babylonians was to seek to brainwash these youths and this was to be done through Babylonian diet and education. These young men wisely asked that they be not fed Babylonian food. Guess being Israelites they knew the above proverb all too well.

Respond:

The Israelites were commanded to observe certain dietary laws as you read in Leviticus 11 and Deuteronomy 14. These laws forbid Jews to eat "unclean" animals like pigs and pelicans. The Law of Moses forbade Jews from ingesting blood or fat.

Without question the King's table was furnished with many foods that the Jewish Law deemed "unclean". This is why Daniel and his friends would not eat them.

RESPONDING TO THE AUTHOR

In Chapter 6 of DANIEL in Babylon, Apostle Michael Scantlebury makes the statements below. Think about each one for a moment, and then respond to the questions/exercises in the spaces provided.

From the Book: *Intoxicating Liquors*

From the Book of Proverbs, Daniel got the idea that those who know and follow the perfect will of God will not drink intoxicating liquors. Look at Proverbs 20:1

1. What is it that Solomon had to say about wine and strong drink in Proverbs 20:1?_____

_____

_____

_____

_____

2. According to Proverbs 23:19-21, 29-35 what does it means to be deceived by intoxicating beverages? _____

_____

_____

_____

---

3. Why would Daniel and his friends not drink the King's wine?

---

4. Did the decision to ask for vegetables and water as their diet instead of what the King had apportioned for their diet come at a risk? _____

From the Book: *The Issue of Vegetables*

"Please test your servants for ten days, and let them give us vegetables to eat and water to drink. [13] Then let our appearance be examined before you, and the appearance of the young men who eat the portion of the king's delicacies; and as you see fit, so deal with your servants." [14] So he consented with them in this matter, and tested them, ten days." Daniel 1:12-14

5. What is it that we need to take away from this account as New Testament, 21st Century Believers? _____

_____

_____

_____

_____

_____

6. Why is it important for us to understand that we serve God in the midst of the corrupting influences of this world's value system? _____

_____

_____

_____

_____

7. What caused these young Jewish prisoners to encounter a fiery furnace and a den full of lions? _____

_____

_____

_____

_____

_____

8. What should be the results of a test into our lives even as Daniel and his friends were tested for ten days? _____

_____

_____

_____

_____

_____

9. Likewise us as _____ in this 21ˢᵗ Century world in which we now live, as we maintain our intense____ and loyalty to Jesus Christ and the Word of God the same would happen to us. Just like Jesus, and the early _____ _____ and all those who came before us, the _____ of the day were always after them. The Scripture admonishes us as: "Yes, and ___ who desire to _____ _____ in Christ Jesus will suffer _____."

From the Book: *Sync between Internal and External*

Daniel 1:12-13 - "Please test your servants for ten days, and let them give us vegetables to eat and water to drink. 13 Then let our appearance be examined before you, and the appearance of the young men who eat the portion of the king's delicacies; and as you see fit, so deal with your servants." This means:

- Our _____ _____ must be _____ in the _____.

- Our _____ _____ and _____ must be _____ to all from the _____.

- Our _____ must be _____.

- This thing _____ _____. This principle of eating _____ must _____ results. It must not just be a _____ _____ it must be _____.

- We must tap into a _____ from a _____ _____.

APPLYING YOUR INSIGHTS

1. Review what you've written and learned in this workbook chapter. As further thoughts or ideas come to mind, list them below. (Include questions or comments that you would like to raise when your small group meets.) _____

---

2. What was the most meaningful concept or truth in this chapter of Daniel in Babylon – The Issue of Vegetables? How will this enrich your life of family, church, or community? ____

---

3. Take some time to pray and intercede — for yourself, your family, your church, your city, and the world. List some of your most pressing needs and requests here: _____

_____

_____

_____

_____

_____

4. Take some time to pray and give thanks. What blessing and joys has God brought into your life this week? Name some of them here? _____

_____

_____

_____

_____

_____

REVIEWING IN THE WORD

Be sure to check out these Scriptures related to the topic of "Issue of Vegetables"

Daniel 1:8-10; 12-14   Proverbs 20:1

Proverbs 23:1-3   Proverbs 23:19-21; 29-35

Matthew 4:1-4   2 Timothy 3:12

FOR GROUP DISCUSSION

In your small group, discuss one or more of the following, as time permits.

1. Use our opening moments to share some of your major insights, comments, or questions from your reading of Chapter 6, The Issue of Vegetables. (Refer to your individual Workbook responses, as well.)

2. Apostle Michael Scantlebury says, "What we need to take away from this account as New Testament believers is the whole issue of survival in a hostile environment. Vegetables must represent that which is opposite to the diet of Babylon, the world system. Vegetables must then represent the word of God". What are your thoughts on this statement?

3. What is meant by "test your Servants"? Have you seen/experienced this principle in carrying out the daily operations among your leaders? In yourself?

4. Read aloud Matthew chapter 4 versus 1 to 4 and discuss as to how it applies to our lives.

5. Can you explain in brief what you understand by "We must understand that as we serve God in the midst of the corrupting influences of this world's value system, our "diet" (Word of God) must work?

****

Close your group time in prayer ......

CHAPTER 7
THE ISSUE OF RESOURCES

Focusing In:

Because Daniel and his companions were drawing from another source than that of the Babylonians they were proven to be far superior after being evaluated. In essence they were saying – We are men of God and we will live according to the things of the Spirit, evaluate us after a period and you would see the difference between us and those who submitted to the king's meat – "the flesh".

— Apostle Michael Scantlebury

Reflect:

In the natural there was no way that these men by eating vegetables and drinking water, rather than the king's meat could have produced the results that were manifested. So where did they gain the results? To whom did they turn in-order to have the results that were expected of them? Can we have similar results over situations in our lives?

Respond: Daniel 1:15-17

> "And at the end of ten days their features appeared better and fatter in flesh than all the young men who ate the portion of the king's delicacies. [16]Thus the steward too away their portion of delicacies and the wine that they were to drink, and gave them vegetables. [17]As for these four young men, God gave them knowledge and skill in all

all literature and wisdom; and Daniel had understanding
in all visions and dreams."

This then indicates a principle that, they were placing the Spiritual
above the natural. From the onset these men set up this principle.

There are Two Realms that Exist:

1.   The Natural Realm

This realm is the dimension that is subject to the laws of time,
space and physical things. It is a dimension that can be accessed
through the physical senses.

2.   The Supernatural Realm

The supernatural realm is the dimension that operates above
natural laws. It is the spiritual realm, which is invisible *(unseen)*,
permanent, and eternal-*it is located outside of time.* The spiritual realm
exercises dominion over the natural realm.

RESPONDING TO THE AUTHOR

In Chapter 7 of DANIEL in Babylon, Apostle Michael
Scantlebury makes the statements below. Think about each one
for a moment, and then respond to the questions/exercises in the
spaces provided.

From the Book: Resources

According to the Webster's English Dictionary resource means
the following:

- A source of supply or support: an available means—usually
  used in the plural.

- A natural source of wealth or revenue—often used in the plural.

- A natural feature or phenomenon that enhances the quality of human life.

- A source of information or expertise.

- Something to which, one has recourse in difficulty.

- In the _____ there was no way that these men by eating _____ and drinking _____, rather than the king's could have produced the _____ that were manifested.

10. According to Daniel 1:15-20 who was their source? _____

_____

_____

_____

_____

_____

11. What does the writer of Romans in Chapter 8:5-9 admonishes us?

_____

_____

_____

_____

From the Book: Set Your Mind

The writer of the Book of Romans admonishes us to live the same way that Daniel and his friends chose to live – to draw from God and live according to the Spirit.

> "For those who live according to the flesh *set their minds* on the things of the flesh, but those who live according to the Spirit, the things of the Spirit. 6 For to be carnally minded is death, but to be spiritually minded is life and peace. 7 Because the carnal mind is enmity against God; for it is not subject to the law of God, nor indeed can be. 8 So then, those who are in the flesh cannot please God. 9 But you are not in the flesh but *in the Spirit*, if indeed the Spirit of God dwells in you. Now if anyone does not have the Spirit of Christ, he is not His." Romans 8:5-9

12. What are the literal meanings of the Greek word translated "set their minds"? _____

_____

_____

_____

_____

_____

13. How can one be in phase with the Spirit and to master and conquer this life? _____

_____

_____

_____

_____

_____

- So let us read this Romans 8 verse 5 again for emphasis – "they who are _____ _____ to be in phase with the _____ will walk according to the _____; but they who _____ to be inn phase or _____ with the _____ will walk in the _____.

14. What is meant by the phrase "in the Sprit" in Romans Chapter 8 verse 9? _____

_____

_____

_____

_____

_____

15. What are we called to be in Galatians 5:25? _____

_____

_____

_____

_____

_____

16. What are the characteristics of the type of love Colossians 1:8 talks about? _____

_____

_____

_____

_____

_____

17. Where does our resource come from according to John 6:1-
68? _____

_____

_____

_____

_____

APPLYING YOUR INSIGHTS

1. Review what you've written and learned in this workbook
   chapter. As further thoughts or ideas come to mind, list them
   below. (Include questions or comments that you would like to
   raise when your small group meets.) _____

_____

_____

_____

_____

2. What was the most meaningful concept or truth in this chapter

of Daniel in Babylon – The Issue of Resources? How will this enrich your life, of family, church, or community?

_____

_____

_____

_____

_____

3. Take some time to pray and intercede — for yourself, your family, your church, your city, and the world. List some of your most pressing needs and requests here: _____

_____

_____

_____

_____

_____

4. Take some time to pray and give thanks. What blessing and joys has God brought into your life this week? Name some of them here? _____

_____

_____

_____

_____

REVIEWING IN THE WORD

Be sure to check out these Scriptures related to the topic of "The Issue of Resources"

Daniel 1: 15-20

Romans 8: 5-9

Galatians 3: 3

Galatians 5: 16, 25

Ephesians 6: 18

Philippians 3: 3

Colossians 1: 8

Hebrews 12: 1-13

John 6: 1-68

FOR GROUP DISCUSSION

In your small group, discuss one or more of the following, as time permits.

1. Use your opening moments to share some of your major insights, comments, or questions from your reading of Chapter 7, The Issue of Resources. (Refer to your individual Workbook responses, as well.)

2. Apostle Michael Scantlebury says, "That this is not the "*sloppy-a-guppy*" kind of love, no, it is tough love. Tough love, for example Hebrews 12:1–13". What are your thoughts on this statement?

3. What does it mean by "in the Spirit"? Do you believe you have seen/experienced this mindset operational in any of your leaders? In yourself?

4. Read aloud Hebrews 12:1-13 and John 6:1-68 and discuss how it apply to our walk as God's called-out today?

5. Can you explain in brief "In essence then, our resource comes from another realm"

****

Close your group time in prayer ......

CHAPTER 8
NEBUCHADNEZZAR'S DREAM AND ITS INTERPRETATION

Focusing In:

As one reads through the Book of Daniel one cannot help but notice/realize that it was in this Book we came to understand for the very first time the concept of The Kingdom of God coming into the earth. At that time Babylon was the strongest kingdom that ever existed. Babylon was stronger than Egypt. It was an impressive kingdom and it was during its existence that God chose to introduce the idea and revelation of His Kingdom and His being much more superior than Babylon and every other kingdom after.

— Apostle Michael Scantlebury

Reflect:

This was not a normal dream therefore king Nebuchadnezzar was so troubled. The dynamic thing about this dream is that he insisted on an interpretation of the dream with ought explaining what exactly he saw. Of course none of his magicians, astrologers, sorcerers or Chaldeans could tell the king what his dream was, nor give its interpretation. Why such unreasonable behavior on the part of the King? Could it be that He was acting on the influence of a greater authority than he was?

Respond:

It was at that point the God of Heaven caused Daniel to be brought to the forefront. He was given both the dream and its interpretation as he called upon the God of Heaven.

All these (magicians, astrologers, sorcerers and Chaldeans) practiced gazing into the future, they were not schooled in the wisdom of God - they were the Babylonian prophets. In this instant they could not interpret because this kairos was fixed to a source. When Babylon failed, Daniel was switched on. Daniel stepped outside of his own natural wisdom and experience and drew from the Resource of God's Holy Spirit and he got the answers.

Daniel 2:31-35-The Dream
   "You, O king, were looking and behold, there was *a single great statue*; that statue, which was large and of extraordinary splendor, was standing in front of you, and its appearance was awesome. 32 The head of that statue was made of fine gold, its breast and its arms of silver, its belly and its thighs of bronze, 33 its legs of iron, its feet partly of iron and partly of clay. 34 You continued looking until *a stone was cut out without hands*, and it *struck the statue on its feet* of iron and clay and crushed them. 35 Then the iron, the clay, the bronze, the silver and the gold were crushed all at the same time and became like chaff from the summer threshing floors; and the wind carried them away so that not a trace of them was found. But the stone that struck the statue became *a great mountain* and filled the whole earth." [Italics added]

RESPONDING TO THE AUTHOR

In Chapter 8 of DANIEL in Babylon, Apostle Michael Scantlebury makes the statements below. Think about each one for a moment, and then respond to the questions/exercises in the spaces provided.

From the Book: *The Interpretation*

"Now we will tell its interpretation before the king. [37] You, O king, are the king of kings, to whom the God of heaven has given the kingdom, the power, the strength and the glory; [38] and wherever the sons of men dwell, or the beasts of the field, or the birds of the sky, He has given them into your hand and has caused you to rule over them all—you *are* this head of gold." Daniel 2:36-38

1. What are the literal meanings of the Greek word "Kairos" used by the author? _____

_____

_____

_____

_____

_____

- One of the certain themes of the _____ of the king's dream was the reality of the _____ of word systems. The _____ of the world against the _____ of God. In the _____ there are several words and phrases that give incredible _____ and _____ as to how the _____ of _____ operates against the _____ of this world. They also reveal the _____ and _____ workings of the kingdoms of this world. Let's take the _____ and _____ them.

- The first thing we see in the dream is that there was an impressive stature; "single great statue". What is the word translated "great" here and what is the meaning of it? _____

2. So what does this "great" looking statue signify in terms of the theme of the dream, which is colliding of the kingdoms? _____

_____

_____

_____

_____

_____

3. What is the Hebrew word translated "great" in the phrase "Became a great mountain"? _____

_____

_____

_____

_____

_____

From the Book: *Comparison to the mountain*

After Daniel spent a considerable amount of time explaining the grandeur of the statue, he then compares it to a mountain. The stone representing The Kingdom of God, unlike the image began small. However, even though it was small it was solid throughout. There was nothing hollow about it. It was acquired from a much greater, rock solid mountain.

4. What do you understand from this above quote? _____

_____

_____

_____

_____

_____

- This _____ was taken out of the _____ but not cut out by any human hands and then it _____ to strike the _____. The Kingdom of God _____ the image and brought it down.

- Impact will always require _____. Every system in the earth that _____ this image will be _____. As a matter of fact _____ _____ this position first in our _____, before, He uses us to _____ the _____ of the earth.

5. What are some of the things that we must realize about the Kingdom of God from the interpretation of this dream? _____

_____

_____

_____

_____

6. The author says "I truly find it interesting that God did not give this revelation to some Pastor in the Church because The Kingdom is not limited to a Church". Do you share this thought with him? Explain. _____

_____

_____

_____

_____

_____

- Daniel continued in his _____ of the king's dream and here is what he revealed about the _____. Remember there were different _____ of the image; thee head was _____, the chest of _____, the legs of _____ and the feet part iron and part _____. He also went on to show that they will _____ but will not _____ to one another. They are joined but not in _____. This is exactly what the _____ of the _____ are today; they seem _____ and _____ but they are _____! We cannot afford to have this aspect of any other aspect of the _____ in the Church, because it seeks to _____ the things of _____ in the Church. It must start on a _____ level and then flow to _____.

From the Book: *The Image Itself*

Let's briefly look at what the image that Nebuchadnezzar saw represented. The Word of God and history have already revealed to us what each aspect of the image represented.

7. What did the different parts of the image represent and what were their strengths and weaknesses? _____

_____

_____

_____

_____

_____

8. In his interpretation Daniel made a very clear statement that cannot be misconstrued when he said: "In the days of these kings the God of Heaven will set up His Kingdom and it shall never be destroyed." What does this mean? _____

_____

_____

_____

_____

_____

9. What does the Hebrew word quwm translated setup in "The God of Heaven will set up His Kingdom" mean? _____

_____

_____

_____

_____

_____

10. What is the emphasis of God's Kingdom? _____

_____

_____

_____

_____

_____

APPLYING YOUR INSIGHTS

1. Review what you've written and learned in this workbook
   chapter. As further thoughts or ideas come to mind, list them
   below. (Include questions or comments that you would like to
   raise when your small group meets.) _____

_____

_____

_____

_____

_____

2. What was the most meaningful concept or truth in this chapter of Daniel in Babylon – King Nebuchadnezzar's dream and it's interpretation? How will this enrich your life, your family, church, or community? _____

_____

_____

_____

_____

_____

3. Take some time to pray and intercede — for yourself, your family, your church, your city, and the world. List some of your most pressing needs and requests here: _____

_____

_____

_____

_____

_____

4. Take some time to pray and give thanks. What blessing and joys has God brought into your life this week? Name some of them here? _____

_____

_____

_____

Reviewing in the Word

Be sure to check out these Scriptures related to the topic of "The Issue of Resources"

Daniel 2: 1-3   Jeremiah 31: 31-40

Daniel 2: 31-35   Ezra 6: 14

Daniel 2: 36-45   Daniel 8: 21, 5-6, 7, 20, 8

For Group Discussion

In your small group, discuss one or more of the following, as time permits.

1. Use your opening moments to share some of your major insights, comments, or questions from your reading of Chapter 8, Nebuchadnezzar's dream and it's interpretation. (Refer to your individual Workbook responses, as well.)

2. Apostle Michael Scantlebury says, "This therefore, lends to the idea that one cannot subscribe to The Kingdom of God and still live lawlessly". What are your thoughts on this statement?

3. What is meant by the terminology used by the author "impact will always require contact"? Do you believe you have seen/experienced this mindset operational in any of your leaders? In yourself?

4. Read aloud Jeremiah 31:31-40 and Daniel 2:44 and discuss what

it means to us today?

5. Can you explain in brief "In the days of these kings the God of Heaven will set up His Kingdom and it shall never be destroyed"

6. Explain your thoughts on the Hebrew word quwam translated setup in "The God of Heaven will setup His Kingdom"

****

Close your group time in prayer ......

CHAPTER 9
THE ISSUE OF PERSECUTION

Focusing In:

Persecution comes from the Hebrew word "radaph" and carries the following shades of meaning: chase, put to flight, follow after, hunt, be under persecution, pursuer. From a primitive root; to run after (usually with hostile intent; figuratively (of time) gone by) -- chase, put to flight, follow (after, on), hunt, (be under) persecute (-ion,-or), pursue (-r).

— Apostle Michael Scantlebury

Reflect:

One may say we live in a society and at a time when we are not persecuted for our "Faith". We live in so called safety and as such we do not need a message on "persecution". However, I am seeing a different level or type of persecution rising in this hour. It is designed to attempt to force The Church/Believer to compromise on the tenets of the written Scripture.

Respond:

Regardless to what the present natural environment is saying we are not first Canadians or Americans or West Indians or Russians or wherever in the earth you are from. We are first Christians; Citizens of Heaven/Kingdom of God and as such the Bible must define who we are, and how we function. Our environment must not shape us; instead we must constantly be defined by the "Word of God".

If we were to listen to the prevailing voice in our region and territory, we would not preach strong lifestyle Christianity. No! Instead we would preach a Gospel of convenience, comfort, all-inclusive regardless of lifestyle, and the list can go on and on.

RESPONDING TO THE AUTHOR

In Chapter 9 of DANIEL in Babylon, Apostle Michael Scantlebury makes the statements below. Think about each one for a moment, and then respond to the questions/exercises in the spaces provided.

From the Book: *Persecution*

We need to fully understand this: PERSECUTION IS A POWERFUL DIMENSION OF THE CHRISTIAN FAITH!

1. What is the literal meaning of the Hebrew word "radaph" translated persecution? _____

_____

_____

_____

_____

- As the author aptly describes we are first _____; Citizens of _____ and as such the _____ must define who we are, and how we _____.

- Remember that the _____ we serve is the same _____, today and forever! We are seeking to

_____ a _____ that would cause us to _____ in any situation of _____.

2. So where in the Word of God can we find the type of mentality we are to construct in order that we may stand strong in the face of persecution? _____

_____

_____

_____

_____

_____

3. What are the principles that we could learn from the experiences of these men? _____

_____

_____

_____

_____

_____

- Therefore, if you are called upon to _____, and even _____ for your _____ in Jesus Christ be _____ to do it.

From the Book: *Apostle Paul's Admonition to Timothy*

"Yes, and all who desire to live godly in Christ Jesus will suffer persecution. 13 But evil men and impostors will grow worse and worse, deceiving and being deceived. 14 But you must continue in the things which you have learned and been assured of, knowing from whom you have learned them, 15 and that from childhood you have known the Holy Scriptures, which are able to make you wise for salvation through faith which is in Christ Jesus. 16 All Scripture is given by inspiration of God, and is profitable for doctrine, for reproof, for correction, for instruction in righteousness, 17 that the man of God may be complete, thoroughly equipped for every good work." 2 Timothy 3: 12-17

4. What do you understand from this portion of Scripture? _____

_____

_____

_____

_____

_____

5. How are we as the called out of God to be made complete and thoroughly equipped for every good work? _____

_____

_____

_____

_____

_____

6. What does the word of God assures we will have to face if we desire to live godly in Christ Jesus? _____

_____

_____

_____

_____

_____

7. What has 1 Corinthians 10:13 to say about the many situations that we will have to face during our life here on earth? _____

_____

_____

_____

_____

- Witness: comes from the _____ word _____ where we derived the word _____. So to be a _____ as a _____ one must take into _____ the idea of being asked to be a _____. This is very serious stuff and cannot be _____ lightly.

From the Book: *Possessing an Excellent Spirit*

"Then this Daniel distinguished himself above the governors and satraps, because an excellent spirit was in him; and the king gave thought to setting him over the whole realm." Daniel 6:3

8. What did this excellent spirit allow Daniel to achieve? _____

_____

_____

_____

_____

_____

- We need this _____ of _____ to operate both in _____ lives and that of our _____. Excellence is not something we do only when things are going _____ and we are not _____ any form of _____ or _____. NO! Excellence is something that we should make an _____ principle of our lives, regardless!

9. From which language is the English word "Patience" derived from? What does it mean? _____

_____

_____

_____

_____

_____

APPLYING YOUR INSIGHTS

1. Review what you've written and learned in this workbook chapter. As further thoughts or ideas come to mind, list them below. (Include questions or comments that you would like to raise when your small group meets.) _____

_____

_____

_____

_____

_____

2. What was the most meaningful concept or truth in this chapter of Daniel in Babylon – The Issue of Persecution? How will this enrich your life, your family, church, or community? _____

_____

_____

_____

_____

_____

3. Take some time to pray and intercede — for yourself, your family, your church, your city, and the world. List some of your most pressing needs and requests here: _____

_____

_____

_____

_____

_____

4. Take some time to pray and give thanks. What blessing and joys has God brought into your life this week? Name some of them here? _____

_____

_____

_____

_____

REVIEWING IN THE WORD

Be sure to check out these Scriptures related to the topic of "The Issue of Persecution"

Daniel 3: 1-27	Daniel 6:1-23
Proverbs 25:26	Luke 21:10-19
Acts 1:8	1 Corinthians 10:13
2 Corinthians 6:2-10	2 Corinthians 11:22-33
2 Thessalonians 1:4-12	1 Timothy 6:11-12
2 Timothy 3:12-17	Hebrews 6:9-12
Hebrews 12:12-13	1 Peter 3:13-18
1 Peter 4:1-8, 12-19	James 1:2-3, 12
James 5:7-11	

FOR GROUP DISCUSSION

In your small group, discuss one or more of the following, as time permits.

1. Use your opening moments to share some of your major insights, comments, or questions from your reading of Chapter 9, The Issue of Persecution. (Refer to your individual Workbook responses, as well.)

2. Apostle Michael Scantlebury says, "However, I would like to encourage that our environment must not shape us, instead, we must constantly be defined by the Word of God. If we listen to the prevailing voice in our region and territory we would not reach strong lifestyle Christianity. No! Instead we would preach a Gospel of convenience, comfort, all-inclusive regardless of lifestyle." What are your thoughts on this statement?

3. What is meant by "possessing an excellent spirit" in Daniel 6:3? Do you believe you have seen/experienced this mindset operational in any of your leaders? In yourself?

4. Read aloud Daniel 3:1-27 and discuss what it means to us today?

5. Can you explain in brief "As we look back at these events, it is quite evident that the plot of the devil was to wipe out these men. However, their experiences reveal to us some very important principles for "walking in the midst of fire."

6. How differently do you view Luke 21:19 now that you have a greater understanding of the word "Patience" in this Scripture, translated from the Greek word "Hupomone"?

****

Close your group time in prayer ......

CHAPTER 10
THE ISSUE OF RULERSHIP

Focusing In:

"One of the significant themes of the Book of Daniel is the issue of Rulership. Babylon was the dominant world power at the time and they used their dominance to invade Israel and take the nation captive. And we have seen before that it was during their exile in Babylon that the God of Heaven moved in giving the king a dream, which he could not remember, nor interpret. Daniel was then given the dream and its interpretation and the whole issue of the dream was the kingdoms of the earth being dismantled and brought under the power and control of the Kingdom of God."

— Apostle Michael Scantlebury

Reflect:

Daniel 4–5 & 7 gives us great commentary and insight into God's heart for His Saints to have dominion in the earth. His plan is for His everlasting Kingdom to rule in the affairs of men upon the earth. His plan is to rule over the kings of the earth.

Respond:

Psalms 2: begins with the statement "Why do the nations rage?" Rage: a plot that is designed to produce chaos. In this context it is a secret conspiracy against God; by hearts that are in violent rebellion against God.

The kings of the earth believe that in rebellion to God, they have the power to rule the earth, but we have news for them. We know that the Word of God is and continues to invade the territories of the earth. (Matthew 28:18–20)

RESPONDING TO THE AUTHOR

In Chapter 10 of DANIEL in Babylon, Apostle Michael Scantlebury makes the statements below. Think about each one for a moment, and then respond to the questions/exercises in the spaces provided.

From the Book: *Rulership over the Kings of the Earth*

The Psalmist David revealed the heart of God in this respect. He penned Psalms 2 to reveal this. Let us briefly explore this Psalm.

1. What is your understanding of this Psalm? Explain in brief. __

_____

_____

_____

_____

_____

2. How does it explain the thought process of the Kings of the Earth? _____

_____

_____

_____

_____

_____

3. What could have prompted the Psalmist to pen those words of admonition for the Kings of this earth? Is there learning for us in those words as God's Ecclesia? _____

_____

_____

_____

_____

_____

4. What has Matthew 28:18-20 to say about our responsibility in establishing God's rule on earth? _____

_____

_____

_____

_____

_____

From the Book: *Dominion and the Purposes of God*

"Also I will make him my firstborn, higher than the kings of the earth." Psalms 89:27

The mere mention of the word higher implies that there exists a stage or a state that is manifestly lower.

1. What is it that we need to take away from this account as New Testament, 21ˢᵗ Century Believers? _____

_____

_____

_____

_____

_____

2. What does the author say will give us the operating power?

_____

_____

_____

_____

_____

From the Book: First-Born Principles

As we explore this, I would like to begin with Romans 12:1-3. I believe it is a very vital part in entering into and walking in the dimension of "the First-Born".

3. Why in your opinion is Apostle Paul beseeching us not to be "*conformed*" to this world? _____

_____

_____

_____

_____

_____

4. Can you explain the meaning of the word "transform" as used
   in the above Scripture? _____

_____

_____

_____

_____

5. What is the relationship between these two words? _____

_____

_____

_____

_____

6. How are we changed as Believers? _____

_____

_____

_____

_____

7. What is the meaning of the word "image" translated from Greek word "suschematizo"? _____

_____

_____

_____

_____

_____

8. What did Jesus declare in John 14:7-11? _____

_____

_____

_____

_____

_____

9. Do you agree with the author's saying, "Just as Christ is the First-Born of God there is a First-Born People? Explain in brief. _____

_____

_____

_____

_____

_____

10. What does the law of the First-Born reveal to us as explained in this chapter through the many biblical references? _____

_____

_____

_____

_____

_____

11. What are five "First-Born Principles" that we could glean from the lives of the Israelites as recorded in the Bible? _____

_____

_____

_____

_____

_____

■ As _____ Believers in _____ _____ we have become God's _____ and all the _____ and _____ of the First-Born _____ to us. Remember that the Scriptures reveal to us that _____ is God's true First-Born:

APPLYING YOUR INSIGHTS

1. Review what you've written and learned in this workbook chapter. As further thoughts or ideas come to mind, list them

below. (Include questions or comments that you would like to raise when your small group meets.) _____

_____

_____

_____

_____

_____

2. What was the most meaningful concept or truth in this chapter of Daniel in Babylon – The Issue of Rulership? How will this enrich your life, your family, church, or community?

_____

_____

_____

_____

_____

3. Take some time to pray and intercede — for yourself, your family, your church, your city, and the world. List some of your most pressing needs and requests here: _____

_____

_____

_____

_____

4. Take some time to pray and give thanks. What blessing and joys has God brought into your life this week? Name some of them here? _____

_____

_____

_____

_____

REVIEWING IN THE WORD

Be sure to check out these Scriptures related to the topic of "The issue of Rulership"

Daniel Chapters 4, 5 & 7	Exodus 12:29-30
Psalms 2:1-12	Exodus 13:1-2, 11-16
Matthew 28:18-20	Numbers 3:5-13, 39-51
Psalms 89:1-37	2 Chronicles 21:3
Romans 12:1-3	Genesis 48:8-20
2 Corinthians 3:18	Deuteronomy 21:15-17
John 14:7-11	Deuteronomy 25:5-10
Colossians 1:15-18	Colossians 1:9-18
Revelations 1:5	Romans 8:28-29
Hebrews 12:18-23	Revelation 1:3-6
Exodus 4:21-23	

FOR GROUP DISCUSSION

In your small group, discuss one or more of the following, as time permits.

1. Use your opening moments to share some of your major insights, comments, or questions from your reading of Chapter 10, The Issue of Rulership. (Refer to your individual Workbook responses, as well.)

2. Apostle Michael Scantlebury says, "Daniel Chapters 4-5 & 7 gives us great commentary and insight into God's heart for His Saints to have dominion in the earth. His plans for His everlasting Kingdom to rule in the affairs of men upon the earth. His plans to rule over the kings of the earth." What are your thoughts on this statement?

3. What is meant by "Being made God's First-Born"? Do you believe this could have an impact on how we carry out our daily operations? Do you see this approach in your leaders? In yourself?

4. Can you explain in brief what you understand by the word "Cloning"? How is this different from being an identical twin? Do you see the cloning of Jesus Christs character traits in your life? In the lives of your leaders and ministry?

5. Read aloud Numbers 3:11-13 and discuss the implications of this Scripture in our lives today.

****

Close your group time in prayer ......

CHAPTER 11
THE ISSUE OF ANTICHRIST

Focusing In:

"This is one of the most controversial topics in all of Christendom so take the time to walk with me through this entire chapter. We are going to look at several passages of Scriptures that deal with antichrist. As I proceed in this chapter I would give you the normal accepted view and look at new revelation that God is giving."

— Apostle Michael Scantlebury

Reflect:

Most Bible scholars and commentators I believe have described the little horn referred to in Daniel 17:8 as the antichrist. However, from the very onset let me hasten to say this, that nowhere in the Bible do we find any mention of the antichrist. There is absolutely no reference to a "single being" referenced as the antichrist. In the two Books (Daniel and Revelation) that many reference when dealing with antichrist, the word or name antichrist is not found. The term antichrist is only found in the Epistles of 1 & 2 John.

Respond:

In their book Victorious Eschatology, Harold Eberle and Martin Trench states "Christians trained in the futurist view envision this passage being fulfilled in the future, before the end of the world. Typically, they think of the abomination of desolation as the antichrist who will walk into the Temple (one that they declare, will be built in the near future) in Jerusalem, set up an idol of himself, and declare himself as God. That event is thought of being a terrible worldwide tribulation."

RESPONDING TO THE AUTHOR

In Chapter 11 of DANIEL in Babylon, Apostle Michael Scantlebury makes the statements below. Think about each one for a moment, and then respond to the questions/exercises in the spaces provided.

From the Book: *Reference to antichrist in the Bible*

> "I was considering the horns, and there was another horn, a little one, coming up among them, before whom three of the first horns were plucked out by the roots. And there, in this horn, were eyes like the eyes of a man, and a mouth speaking pompous words." Daniel 7:8

Most Bible scholars and commentators I believe have described the little horn referred to above in Daniel 7:8 as the antichrist. However, from the very onset let me hasten on to say this, that nowhere in the Bible do we find any mention of *the* antichrist. There is absolutely no reference to a "single being" referenced as the antichrist. In the two Books (Daniel and Revelation) that many reference when dealing with antichrist, the word or name antichrist is not found.

1. What are the Scriptures where the term antichrist appears?

_____

_____

_____

_____

2. What do you understand from these Scriptures? Explain in Brief.

_____

_____

_____

_____

_____

From the Book: *Jesus' Resurrection*

Apostle John was making it abundantly clear how antichrist spirit functions. One would have to appreciate that at the time he was speaking to the idea of a brand *new creation* called Christians or the Church. This was the time when God was setting the stage for the complete destruction of the Old Covenant Temple and the establishing of His New Covenant Temple, the Church (the Body of Jesus Christ). Jesus had recently died and rose from the dead and ascended into Heaven but there were many who did not believe that He rose again and therefore were saying that He was not from God. As a matter there was a vicious rumour perpetrated by the Roman soldiers and some of the Jewish officials in those days that Jesus' Disciples came and stole His Body: Matthew 28:11-15

3. How can we identify the spirit of antichrist? _____

_____

_____

_____

_____

4. What is the warning Jesus gave His Disciples during the renowned Olivet Discourse? _____

_____

_____

_____

_____

_____

5. What is your understanding of Matthew 24:15-28? _____

_____

_____

_____

_____

6. Do you agree with authors Harold Eberle and Martin Trench's understanding and explanation of the above Passage of Scripture? Why or Why Not – Explain in Brief.

_____

_____

_____

_____

7. What are the parallels that could be drawn between the recordings of the Olivet Discourse by Disciples Matthew, Mark and Luke? _____

_____

_____

_____

_____

_____

8. Who did Jesus say should flee Judea according to the Gospels of Matthew, Mark and Luke? _____

_____

_____

_____

_____

From the Book: *The Abomination in the Holy Place*

Now we need to examine what Jesus was referring to when He warned the Disciples about an abomination of desolation standing in the Holy Place.

9. What does the futurist theory tell us that the "Abomination of Desolation" is? _____

_____

_____

_____

_____

10. What do the Gospels have to say about the antichrist? _____

_____

_____

_____

_____

11. Who did Jesus say would be the witnesses of these events?

_____

_____

_____

_____

12. Where is this abomination of desolation to stand? Explain
    how both Apostles Matthew and Luke are correct in their
    reference to this place? _____

_____

_____

_____

_____

_____

13. What is the abomination of desolation? Explain. _____

_____

_____

_____

_____

14. Why was it necessary for the Jews to flee Jerusalem and Judea in such a hurry? _____

_____

_____

_____

_____

15. Do you believe that the events recorded in Matthew 24:15-26 has already taken place? Explain. _____

_____

_____

_____

APPLYING YOUR INSIGHTS

1. Review what you've written and learned in this workbook chapter. As further thoughts or ideas come to mind, list them below. (Include questions or comments that you would like to raise when your small group meets.) _____

_____

_____

_____

_____

2. What was the most meaningful concept or truth in this chapter of Daniel in Babylon – The Issue of Antichrist? How will this enrich your life, your family, church, or community?

_____

_____

_____

_____

3. Take some time to pray and intercede — for yourself, your family, your church, your city, and the world. List some of your most pressing needs and requests here: _____

_____

_____

_____

_____

_____

4. Take some time to pray and give thanks. What blessing and joys has God brought into your life this week? Name some of them here? _____

_____

_____

_____

_____

REVIEWING IN THE WORD

Be sure to check out these Scriptures related to the topic of "The Issue of Antichrist"

Daniel 7:8	Luke 21:5-11
Daniel 9:26	Luke 21:20-21
Matthew 23:1-35	Acts 7:44-50
Matthew 23:37-24:2	Acts 17:22-25
Matthew 24:3-7	1 Corinthians 6:19
Matthew 24:14-28	2 Corinthians 6:16
Matthew 28:11-15	Ephesians 2:19-22
Mark 12:38-40	1 John 2:18-19

122

Mark 13:1-8	1 John 2:22
Mark 13:10	1 John 4:1-3
Mark 13:14	2 John 2:18
Luke 20:45-47	

FOR GROUP DISCUSSION

In your small group, discuss one or more of the following, as time permits.

1. Use your opening moments to share some of your major insights, comments, or questions from your reading of Chapter 11, The Issue of Antichrist. (Refer to your individual Workbook responses, as well.)

2. Apostle Michael Scantlebury says, "Apostle John further states that the spirit of antichrist is one of deception. Having said that, it is undeniable that since the birth, death, burial, resurrection and ascension of Jesus Christ there have been many "antichrists". Even to this day antichrists are still very active!" What are your thoughts on this statement?

3. What is meant by the Greek word "hagios topos" translated Holy Place in Matthew 24? How does this change your view of what this Scripture is conveying? Do you believe this could have an impact on how we carry out our daily operations? Do you see this approach in your leaders? In yourself?

4. According to Scriptural references what is the "abomination of desolation"? Does it have a bearing on us today?

5. Read aloud Ephesians 2:19-22 and discuss the implications of this Scripture in our lives today.

****

Close your group time in prayer ......

CHAPTER 12
THE STONE: THE KINGDOM OF GOD

Focusing In:

God has always been and will always be King, and there has and always will be His Kingdom. But this one Kingdom appears in different ways at different times-it appears one way with Adam and Eve, another way with Abraham. It is transformed again with the nation of Israel, and transformed again with Jesus and the Church.

— Apostle Michael Scantlebury

Reflect:

Jesus could not have come to earth any time earlier, because 'the fullness of time' had not yet come. It was very important that Jesus was born when the last of the four major world kingdoms was in full operation. In the Book of Daniel we read about Babylon one of the greatest empires that ever existed and the dream that Daniel had to interpret, and for the first time we see plainly the mention of The Kingdom of God manifesting in the earth.

Respond:

The term Kingdom denotes God's Purpose-which, is the extension of God's rule. The term Church denotes the present instrument by which that purpose shall be realized; thus the Church is the instrument, vehicle and means of The Kingdom. The Kingdom then by extension is the propagating of the Gospel in bringing others to Christ. And that is done by the Church.

I believe that the very core of The Kingdom is a relationship with Jesus Christ; the King of The Kingdom! However, while this is so some have tried to make it a program! Remember that the Church was added to daily in the Book of Acts. The Kingdom moved forward because of the early Church filling the mandate of God's purpose.

RESPONDING TO THE AUTHOR

In Chapter 12 of DANIEL in Babylon, Apostle Michael Scantlebury makes the statements below. Think about each one for a moment, and then respond to the questions/exercises in the spaces provided.

From the Book: *The Kingdom of God is not the Church*

Jesus first used the word Church in Matthew Chapter 16 to introduce a whole new dynamic to His early Apostles. That word Church as we illustrated earlier comes from the Greek word Ecclesia, which was referred to or meant the Roman Senate.

1. What is the Greek word translated Church? What meaning does it convey? _____

_____

_____

_____

_____

2. What is the Greek word translated Kingdom? What meaning does it convey?

_____

_____

_____

_____

_____

From the Book: *The Arrival of the King of the Kingdom on Earth*

Apostle Paul in writing to the Galatians revealed this: Galatians 4:4

"But when the fullness of the time had come, God sent forth His Son, born of a woman, born under the law…"

3. What is meant by "When the fullness of the time had come"?

_____

_____

_____

_____

4. How many major Empires were spoken about in the interpretation of the dream in Daniel 2:31-45 to the King? What were these Empires? _____

_____

_____

_____

_____

5. What was the uniqueness of the Roman Empire? _____

_____

_____

_____

_____

_____

6. Why was it necessary for the Roman system of Governance to be fully established before the appearance of the King of The Kingdom? _____

_____

_____

_____

_____

_____

7. What resulted as a consequence of Jesus being introduced as "King" and not "Priest" on His arrival on earth? _____

_____

_____

_____

_____

8. How can we conclude that Jesus' priority was to preach about the Kingdom of God? _____

_____

_____

_____

_____

_____

From the Book: *Misconceptions about the Kingdom of God*

The Kingdom of God as aptly described and revealed by Daniel came to destroy all other kingdoms and to grow and grow until it fills the entire earth!

9. What are the two spiritually existent kingdoms on earth today? How do they contrast from one another? _____

_____

_____

_____

_____

_____

10. How can someone become a part of The Kingdom of God?

_____

_____

_____

_____

_____

11. What strategy does the devil use in governance of the kingdom of darkness? _____

_____

_____

_____

_____

_____

12. What are some of the misconceptions of The Kingdom of God?

_____

_____

_____

_____

_____

13. How has each of these misconceptions affected Christianity? Explain in brief. _____

_____

_____

_____

From the Book: The Kingdom – priority in the Life and Ministry of Jesus Christ

As Jesus Christ was baptized and started His earthly ministry He preached The Kingdom of God, because He was the King of The Kingdom. He only spoke about Church twice and that was due to the fact He had to establish His Senate to run the affairs of His Kingdom while He went back to Heaven. So it is very clear to see that The Kingdom of God held priority in the Life and Ministry of Jesus.

- Many _____ take pride in separating _____ and _____ and see the two as opposing _____ with no common _____. However, that was not what Jesus Christ _____ for His _____. He wanted His _____ to advance His _____ rule into every _____ of _____! That has been His _____ and it still is!

14. What are the characteristics of a Kingdom including the Kingdom of God? _____

15. How do these distinct characteristics ascribe to The Kingdom of God? _____

_____

_____

_____

_____

_____

16. Where in the Bible is the Constitution of the Kingdom being explained? _____

_____

_____

_____

_____

17. Who is expected to obey the laws of the Kingdom and what will be the consequence of not obeying these laws? _____

_____

_____

_____

_____

18. What is the purpose of the Army of God? _____

_____

_____

_____

_____

_____

19. What is the Kingdom's Code of Ethics? _____

_____

_____

_____

_____

_____

20. How and when do we demonstrate the Culture of the Kingdom? _____

_____

_____

_____

_____

_____

21. Where do Ambassadors operate? Is this true of us as Ambassadors for Jesus Christ? _____

_____

_____

_____

_____

_____

22. What are some of the most pertinent points about an Ambassador that we need to know in-order to function effectively? _____

- As a matter of fact, the moment someone _____ Jesus Christ as _____ and Lord, the Holy Spirit is at work _____ any trace of that image in that person's life. It starts _____ but _____ until the King of The Kingdom _____ in the heart. The Kingdom of God is highly _____, and as such God and His Word will _____ confront and _____ us to change. The Kingdom of God has the power to completely _____ us. The rock (representing The Kingdom of God) struck and all entities (Gold, Silver, Bronze, Iron and Clay) _____ at the same time! The Kingdom of God will always _____ itself to be _____ to all of the world's _____. That is the _____ of The Kingdom of God!

23. What needs to happen for the Church to be seen from a completely different view? _____

_____

_____

_____

_____

_____

APPLYING YOUR INSIGHTS

1. Review what you've written and learned in this workbook
   chapter. As further thoughts or ideas come to mind, list them
   below. (Include questions or comments that you would like to
   raise when your small group meets.) _____

_____

_____

_____

_____

_____

2. What was the most meaningful concept or truth in this
   chapter of Daniel in Babylon – The Stone: The Kingdom of
   God? How will this enrich your life, your family, church, or
   community? _____

_____

_____

_____

_____

_____

3. Take some time to pray and intercede — for yourself, your
   family, your church, your city, and the world. List some of
   your most pressing needs and requests here: _____

_____

_____

_____

_____

_____

4. Take some time to pray and give thanks. What blessings and
    joys has God brought into your life this week? Name some of
    them here? _____

_____

_____

_____

_____

_____

REVIEWING IN THE WORD

Be sure to check out these Scriptures related to the topic of "The
Stone: The Kingdom of God"

Exodus 19:5-6	Matthew 21:33-45
Deuteronomy 18:15-16	Matthew 18:23
Psalm 138:2	Luke 1:26-33
Psalm 145:10-13	Luke 4:42-43
Isaiah 5:40-43	Luke 4:43-44
Isaiah 9:6-7	Luke 8:1
Daniel 2:31-47	Luke 9:11
Daniel 7:13-28	Luke 12:31

Daniel 12:1-7

Matthew 1:18-25

Matthew 2:1-3

Matthew 3:1-3

Matthew 4:17

Matthew 5:21-24

Matthew 6:10

Matthew 6:33

Matthew 10:7

Matthew 12:28

Matthew 13:24-30

Matthew 13:37-43

Matthew 21:42-44

Matthew 22:1-10

Matthew 24:14-28

Mark 1:14-15

Mark 12:10

Mark 18:17

Luke 16:16-17

Luke 17:20-21

Luke 20:17

Luke 22:29

John 3:3-5

John 18:33-38

John 19:12-13

Acts 1:1-9

Romans 9:33

1 Corinthians 15:12-26

1 Corinthians 10:24-33

2 Corinthians 4:3-4

Ephesians 2:12

2 Thessalonians 2:3

1 Peter 2:6-9

1 John 2:15-17

Revelation 11:15-18

Revelation 17

FOR GROUP DISCUSSION

In your small group, discuss one or more of the following, as time permits.

1. Use your opening moments to share some of your major insights, comments, or questions from your reading of Chapter 12, The Stone: The Kingdom of God. (Refer to your individual Workbook responses, as well.)

2. Apostle Michael Scantlebury says, "The Israelites as a people misunderstood the Promise and made themselves the object of the Promise rather than the conduit for it. Because of that mentality they became very pious and self-righteous and instead of welcoming the Messiah they rejected Him when He came to earth." What are your thoughts on this statement?

3. What is meant when in the dream about the statue it is revealed that the elements of the great statue "will combine but will not adhere"? How does this change your view of our job as Ambassadors for Jesus Christ? Do you believe this could have an impact on how we carry out our daily operations? Do you see this approach in your leaders? In yourself?

4. What is the Greek word translated "world" in 1 Corinthians 10:24-33 and what is the meaning of it? How does it change your perspective of what this portion of Scripture is telling us? Does it call for a change in the way you operate at present?

5. What was the significant difference in the way the Roman Empire invaded and concurred a country that parallels God's expectation from us in extending His Kingdom on earth?

6. Read aloud Matthew Chapters 6-7 and discuss the implications of this Scripture in our lives today.

****

Close your group time in prayer ......

CHAPTER 13
THE RETURN OF THE KING OF THE KINGDOM

Focusing In:

The Eschatological view that I believe the Bible speaks about shows that The Kingdom of God will grow and advance until it fills the earth. The Church will rise in unity, maturity, and glory before the return of Jesus.

I believe the way we understand and view life and the times in which we live will dictate how we build. In essence if we have an incorrect Eschatology we would place emphasis on the wrong things and thereby build inaccurately.

— Apostle Michael Scantlebury

Reflect:

One of the things that most Christians keep missing is the simple fact that the Holy Scriptures was written for us but not to us. The New Testament was written to the Jews to signal the end of the Old Covenant and the establishment of the New Covenant. The New Testament was also written to the 1st Century Believers as to how the New Nation called the Church should live in relation to Almighty God. As such the New Testament is written for us to draw from so that we could live righteously before God in the earth.

Respond:

In light of this we could begin to understand that much of what is in the Bible has already been fulfilled and the challenge that exists is to accurately discover what has been fulfilled and what remains to be fulfilled. I believe that there are only three major things remaining to be fulfilled from the writings of Scripture, which are:

1. The physical and bodily return of Jesus Christ, The King.

2. The resurrection of the dead.

3. The final judgment.

RESPONDING TO THE AUTHOR

In Chapter 13 of DANIEL in Babylon, Apostle Michael Scantlebury makes the statements below. Think about each one for a moment, and then respond to the questions/exercises in the spaces provided.

From the Book: *The Final Return of Jesus Christ the King*

Some of you reading this chapter may ask why the final return of Jesus Christ rather than the Second Coming. Here is why: There has been much debate and confusion surrounding the statements Jesus made in Matthew Chapter 24 and the time He was referring to them being fulfilled. Many reading Matthew Chapter 24 read it with a futuristic lens view and not with a 1st Century lens view, not realizing that it was written to a 1st Century audience. As a result there has been much controversy trying to fit most, if not all of that Chapter's discourse into the 21st Century or some future time. Let's take a brief moment and explore a few of those conflicts and bring some clarity to them.

▪ With all this talk of The Kingdom _____ in the, the Church

being _____, and satan not taking over, this
requires a major _____ _____ for many readers.
Quite frequently this shift _____ the same questions to
the _____ in the minds of those _____ with it. I
(Jonathan) am asked this same question very often: "If
there is no _____, no future _____ _____,
and no _____, then do you believe in the _____
of Jesus Christ?" The answer is absolutely yes!

1. According to the Authors Jim Wies and Jonathan Welton a lot
   of the verses that speak of Jesus' coming on the clouds of
   heaven are actually about the AD 70 destruction of Jerusalem.
   Do you agree with them as do Apostle Michael Scantlebury?
   Why or Why not – Explain in detail? _____

_____

_____

_____

_____

_____

2. According to your understanding, which of the Bible
   prophesies are still to be fulfilled? _____

_____

_____

_____

_____

_____

3. What were the three major Bible prophesies that the Early Church leaders who gathered in Nicaea in AD 325 agreed are still to be fulfilled? _____

_____

_____

_____

_____

4. What was Jesus referring to when He used the Hebrew phrase "coming upon clouds"? _____

_____

_____

_____

_____

5. Do you believe Jesus also referred to a future time when He would physically return to earth? Explain with scriptural references. _____

_____

_____

_____

_____

From the Book: *The Resurrection of the Dead*

The Resurrection is one of the foundational pillars of the Gospel and the Christian Church! It was so important that it was one of the main topics of the early Apostles' teachings. When they preached they always testified concerning the Resurrection of Jesus Christ, and the consequent resurrection of the dead. As a matter of fact the Resurrection of Jesus Christ in bodily form was so important that when the remaining Eleven Apostles had to choose another Apostle to replace Judas Iscariot who became apostate, they knew that the replacement had to have witnessed the Resurrection of Jesus Christ. (Read Acts 1:15-26)

6. What caused the Apostles Peter and John to be imprisoned according to Acts 4:1-3? _____

_____

_____

_____

_____

_____

7. What stirred the curiosity of the Athenians when Apostle Paul preached among them? What was their response? _____

_____

_____

_____

_____

_____

8. What caused a great dispute and division among the Pharisees

and the Sadducees of the Sanhedrin council when Apostle Paul started to testify of his faith? _____

_____

_____

_____

_____

_____

9. What are we referring to when we speak about the Resurrection of the dead? _____

_____

_____

_____

_____

_____

10. What is God's original plan, which is still relevant today? _____

_____

_____

_____

_____

_____

11. Can this plan/desire of God be the reason for the necessity for a resurrection? Explain. _____

_____

_____

_____

_____

_____

12. What does the mention of Joseph's bones in Hebrews 11:23 have to do with faith? _____

_____

_____

_____

_____

_____

13. How will you explain a whole chapter in the Book of Genesis being dedicated to describing the details of Abraham purchasing a burial ground for his family south of Jerusalem?

_____

_____

_____

_____

_____

14. What could have been the reason for Joseph to desire and instruct that his bones be taken and deposited in the family burial grounds? _____

_____

_____

_____

_____

_____

■ I believe with all my heart that the Prophet _____ was among those who walked the streets of _____ that day, as well as _____, _____, and _____. Why else did the Spirit lead them to make their _____ place _____, almost on the outskirts of that city where all this was taking place? So what is the result? Many _____ of Saints, _____ all the New Testament Church who have gone on to be with the Lord are still in the _____ today, _____ for the _____. Then shall they be _____ upon with life, and then shall _____ be swallowed up in _____! This is our _____ as Saints, and we are looking ever onward to that blessed hope. But there were some who did not have to wait until the final _____ for their _____ bodies to put on _____. Up to now, they have been enjoying their glorified bodies for almost 2000 years. Why? Because they were men and women of faith, Saints, "set apart," to be joined to Jesus Christ as the "First Fruits" of them who slept. (1 Corinthians 15:20)

15. How does this whole message affect us today? _____

_____

_____

_____

_____

_____

16. What are the 2 main issues concerning the resurrection, around which there is much debate? _____

_____

_____

_____

_____

17. What are the views of the small but growing group of Saints called the full Preterists? _____

_____

_____

_____

_____

18. How will you respond to the beliefs of the full Preterists?

_____

_____

_____

_____

_____

- There are some who _____ that Apostle _____ reference to the "spiritual body" speaks of the _____ of the body- its _____ makeup. Consequently, they are _____ to employ this verse for _____ a _____ _____. Of course, this is as wrong-headed as to say a Coca-Cola bottle is made of Coca-Cola. Note the following _____ supporting the _____ approach to Apostle Paul's _____

19. With the aid of Scripture explain why you do or do not agree with this belief? _____

_____

_____

_____

_____

_____

- Apostle Paul's _____ and _____ show that his concern is not _____ over _____, but _____ over _____ (verse 42), _____ over _____ (verse 43a), and _____ over _____ (verse 43b). Our resurrected _____ is so _____ by the _____ _____ that the _____ of our _____ condition will be _____ overcome by the _____ power of the Spirit. Indeed, he _____ the _____ of _____ as the _____.

20. How does, the scholars, A.T. Robertson and N.T. Wright supports the historic faith of the Church regarding the resurrection? _____

From the Book: *The Final Judgment*

Many verses throughout the New Testament clearly teach about the Final Judgment, including these Words from Jesus:

> "And he has given him authority to judge because he is the Son of Man. Do not be amazed at this, for a time is coming when all who are in their graves will hear his voice and come out — those who have done what is good will rise to live, and those who have done what is evil will rise to be condemned." John 5:27-29

21. What do you believe this Scripture is saying to us? _____

_____

_____

_____

_____

_____

22. What is the difference between the phrase Jesus "coming in His glory" and the Hebrew idiom "coming in clouds"? _____

_____

_____

_____

_____

_____

23. How are Christians expected to be rewarded for their individual work/conduct? _____

_____

_____

_____

_____

_____

24. Does the Bible talk about a certain time period during which this Final Judgment is to take place? Is there anything we can do in hastening the return of Christ as King? _____

_____

_____

_____

_____

25. How can we conclude that the popular notion "Jesus could return at any moment" is not a sound doctrine of the Bible?

_____

_____

_____

_____

_____

26. How can we conclude that the popular notion "Jesus could return at any moment" is not a sound doctrine of the Bible? For what purpose is the "Any-Moment" return Scriptures recorded in the Bible? Do they have a relevance to us today?

_____

_____

_____

_____

_____

27. What kind of practical advice did Jesus leave behind for His followers to be able to avoid the catastrophe, which was eminent in their day? _____

_____

_____

_____

_____

_____

28. What are the instructions for us today? What are we to be doing until Jesus' return to earth as King? _____

_____

_____

_____

_____

_____

- Let's review. So far in this chapter we have _____ that Jesus came to _____ as the _____ over all _____. He _____ His Kingdom, and it began to _____ from the _____ _____ onwards to this _____ day. He also _____ the _____ to be ___ _____ and that the _____ is _____ _____ to _____ _____ His Kingdom in the _____.

29. What is the ultimate mandate of the Church of Jesus Christ?

_____

_____

_____

_____

30. How is this to assist in the return of Jesus Christ back to earth as King of Kings? _____

_____

_____

_____

_____

31. Will there be salvations going on forever? _____

_____

_____

_____

_____

_____

32. What are the reasons for supposing that the Church was not taken during the destruction of the Temple in AD 70 and that the Marriage Supper of the Lamb has not already taken place?

_____

_____

_____

_____

_____

33. Why is the grace gifting of Apostles and Prophets so important to the Church? _____

_____

_____

_____

_____

_____

APPLYING YOUR INSIGHTS

1. Review what you've written and learned in this workbook
    chapter. As further thoughts or ideas come to mind, list them
    below. (Include questions or comments that you would like to
    raise when your small group meets.) _____

    _____

    _____

    _____

    _____

2. What was the most meaningful concept or truth in this
    chapter of Daniel in Babylon – The return of the King of the
    Kingdom? How will this enrich your life, your family, church,
    or community? _____

    _____

    _____

    _____

    _____

3. Take some time to pray and intercede — for yourself, your
    family, your church, your city, and the world. List some of
    your most pressing needs and requests here: _____

    _____

_____

_____

_____

_____

4. Take some time to pray and give thanks. What blessings and joys has God brought into your life this week? Name some of them here? _____

_____

_____

_____

_____

REVIEWING IN THE WORD

Be sure to check out these Scriptures related to the topic of "The Return of the King of The Kingdom.

Genesis 49:29-32	Acts 22:29-30
Genesis 50:24-26	Acts 23:1, 6-8
Exodus 13:19	Romans 1:11
Psalm 18:9-12	1 Corinthians 2:13-15
Psalm 68:18	1 Corinthians 3:1
Psalm 104:2-3	1 Corinthians 3:12-15
Isaiah 19:1	1 Corinthians 10:3-4
Joel 2:1-2	1 Corinthians 12:1

154

Nahum 1:3

Zephaniah 1:14-15

Matthew 6:10

Matthew 24:3b

Matthew 24:15-18

Matthew 24:30

Matthew 24:42

Matthew 25:13

Matthew 25:31-33, 46

Matthew 27:51-53

Mark 13:33

John 5:27-29

Acts 1:9-11

Acts 1:15-26

Acts 2:31

Acts 2:46

Acts 4:1-3

Acts 4:23, 32-37

Acts 6:13-14

Acts 17:16-19

Acts 17:31-32

Acts 19:9

Romans 8:1-7

Romans 8:11

1 Corinthians 15:12-38, 42-45, 50-54

2 Corinthians 5:18-20

Ephesians 1:3

Ephesians 2:14-22

Ephesians 3:1-11

Ephesians 4:11-16

Ephesians 5:19

Galatians 6:1

Colossians 1:9

1 Thessalonians 4:13-18

1 Thessalonians 5:6b

Titus 2:13

Hebrews 9:28

Hebrews 11:1-2, 13-40

James 4:13-17

James 5:1-9

Revelation 20:11-15

Revelation 22:10-13

Revelation 22:16-21

For Group Discussion

In your small group, discuss one or more of the following, as time permits.

1. Use your opening moments to share some of your major insights, comments, or questions from your reading of Chapter 13, The Return of the King of the Kingdom. (Refer to your individual Workbook responses, as well.)

2. Apostle Michael Scantlebury says, "The Foundation of the Church of Jesus Christ has already been laid and no one can change that. However, it is absolutely clear that there is still need for Apostles, Prophets, Evangelists, Pastors and Teachers functioning in the Church. We cannot afford to take one or some and omit the others. The Five-Fold Ministry is a complete package that is to be functional until Jesus returns for His Mature Bride!" What are your thoughts on this statement?

3. Why was it important for the first generation Church to be alert and watchful where as it is not so for us today?

4. In 1 Corinthians 3: 12-15 Apostle Paul talks about a rewarding of the Saints at the final judgement. Do you believe understanding this biblical truth could have an impact on how we carry out our daily operations? Do you see this approach in your leaders? In yourself?

5. What is the Greek word translated "see" in Ephesians 3:9 and what is the meaning of it? How does it change your perspective of the need for the Five-Fold Ministry in the Church today? Does it call for a change in the way you think and operate at present?

6. What do you understand from Mathew 24:30 where Jesus talks about His coming: "And then the sign of the Son of Man will appear in the sky, and then all the tribes of the earth will mourn, and they will see the SON OF MAN COMING ON THE CLOUDS OF THE SKY with power and great glory"?

7. Read aloud Romans Chapter 8:1-7 and discuss the implications of this Scripture in our lives today.

****

Close your group time in prayer ......

Further Thoughts

FURTHER THOUGHTS

FURTHER THOUGHTS

FURTHER THOUGHTS

FURTHER THOUGHTS

FURTHER THOUGHTS

Further Thoughts

Further Thoughts

Other Exciting Titles

By Michael Scantlebury

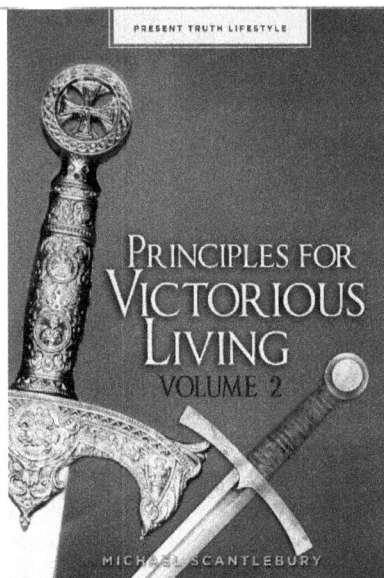

Principles For Victorious Living Volume II

The initial purpose of the five-fold ministry is for the perfecting or maturing of the Saints, which leads to its next intention, which is the real work of the ministry of Jesus Christ, reconciling the world back to the Father. This book lends itself to help in the maturing of the Saints. It adds insight and strategies that help in achieving exponential personal growth preparing one for the real work of the ministry. This is a volume of information and revelation needed in such a time as this, when maturity and focus are the needed key components that bring us an overcoming victory in this realm and advance the Kingdom of God.

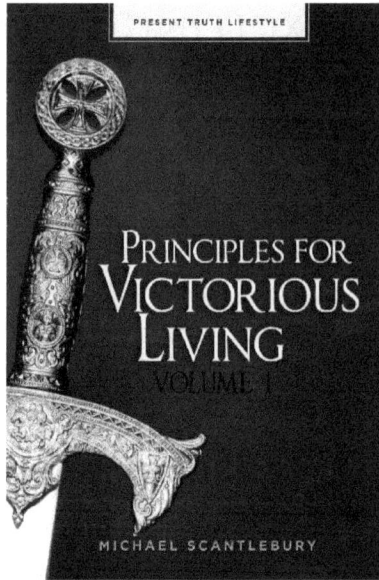

Principles For Victorious Living Vol I

The information contained herein is well balanced with a spiritual maturity that keenly stems from wisdom and revelation in the knowledge of Christ. This is the anointing of an Apostle, and the truths that our brother shares will certainly cause you to excel in the Kingdom of God long before this life is over when later we enter the eternals. There's so much to experience today in this life, and Michael extracts so much from the Word of God to facilitate that. His insight of revelation and ability to interpret and articulate what his spirit receives from the Lord are powerful.

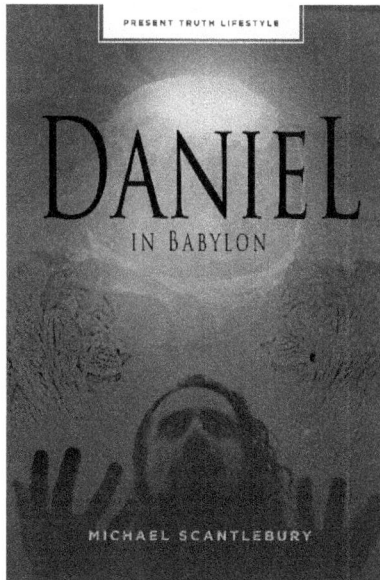

Present Truth Lifestyle – Daniel In Babylon

This is a seminal study with strong Apostolic messaging, yet its flowing style allows for easy assimilation of biblical truths, and provides accurate insights for the cerebral believer, who like Daniel and his companions, are usually the target of the world system. In this book various methodologies are outlined through which, spiritual Babylon seeks to entice the brightest and best of every Godly generation, to acculturize, rob of spiritual identity and manipulate to promote world kingdom end.

But thanks be to God, there is still a generation in the earth spiritually alert enough to operate within the world system, yet deploy their talents and giftings to bring honour and glory to God. Those with the Daniel mindset will decode dreams and visions and interpret judgements written on the kingdoms of this world in this season.

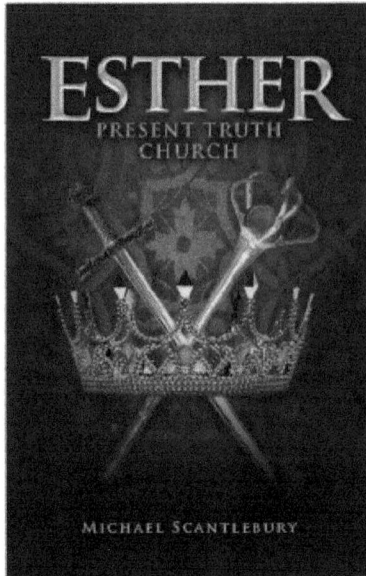

Esther Present Truth Church

In a season where the Church co-exists harmoniously with truth and error, this book provides us with a precision tool and well-calibrated instrument of change that is able to fine-tune the global Body of Christ.

The Book of Esther is rich with revelation that is still valid and applicable for the day in which we live. Hidden within its pages is a powerful "present truth" message. The lives of the people involved and the conditions that are seen have spiritual parallels for the Church. Our destiny as the Body of Christ is revealed. The preparations and conditions we must attain to are all similar.

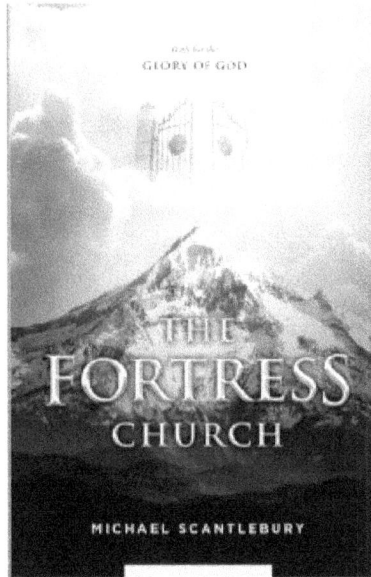

The Fortress Church

According to Webster's English Dictionary "fortress" is defined as: a fortified place: stronghold, *especially*: A large and permanent fortification sometimes including a town. A place that is protected against attack. This book seeks to describe what is a "Fortress Church". We would be looking into the dynamics of this Church as described in Jacob's vision in Genesis Chapter 28, also as described by the Prophet Isaiah, in Isaiah Chapter 2 and as the one detailed in a Psalm of the sons of Korah in Psalms Chapter 48. We would also be looking at a working model of this type of church as found at Antioch in the Book of Acts. Finally we would be exploring The Church at Ephesus, where the Apostle Paul by the Holy Spirit revealed some powerful descriptions of The Church.

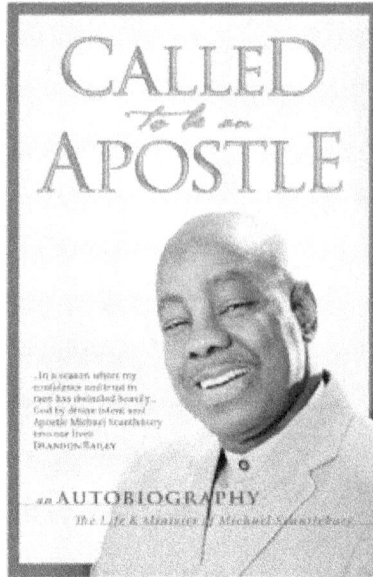

Called To Be An Apostle

This autobiography spans fifty-two years of my life on the earth thus far and I have the hope of living several more... Our home was always packed with young people and we did enjoy times of really wonderful fellowship! Although we were experiencing these wonderful times of fellowship my appetite and desire to grow in the things of God continued unabated. I continued to read anything and everything that I could put my hands on that would strengthen my life. I began reading Wigglesworth, Moody, Finney, Idahosa, Lake, and the list went on and on! But the more I read the more this question burned in my heart—"*why is it that every time we hear/read about a move of God, it is always miles away and in another country? Why can't I experience some of the things that I am reading about?*" Little did I know the Lord would answer that desire!

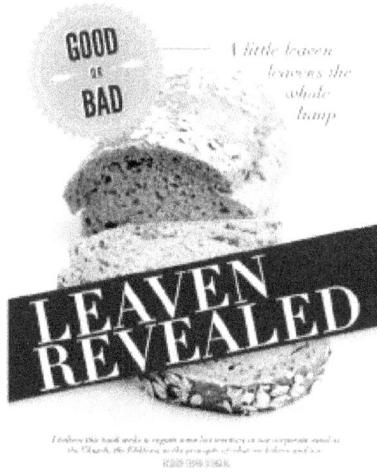

Leavened Revealed

The Bible has a lot to say about *leaven* and its effects upon the Believer. Leaven as an ingredient gives a false sense of growth. In the New Testament there are at least six types of *leaven* spoken about and we will be exploring them in detail, in order to ensure that our lives are completely free of the first five, and completely influenced by the sixth! These types of leaven include the following: The leaven of the Pharisees; The leaven of the Sadducees; The leaven of the Galatians; The leaven of Herod; The leaven of the Corinthians. However, the Leaven of the Kingdom of God is the only type of leaven that has the power and capacity to bring about true growth and lasting change to our lives.

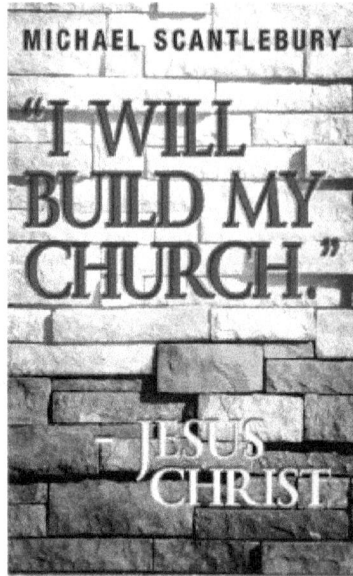

I Will Build My Church – Jesus Christ

"For we are his *masterpiece*, created in Christ Jesus for good works
that God prepared long ago to be our way of life." Ephesians 2:10

What a powerful picture of The Church of Jesus Christ—His Masterpiece! Reference to a *masterpiece* lends to the idea that there are other pieces and among them all, this particular one stands head and shoulders above the rest! This is so true when it comes to The Church that Jesus Christ is building; when you place it alongside everything else that God has created, The Church is by far His Masterpiece!

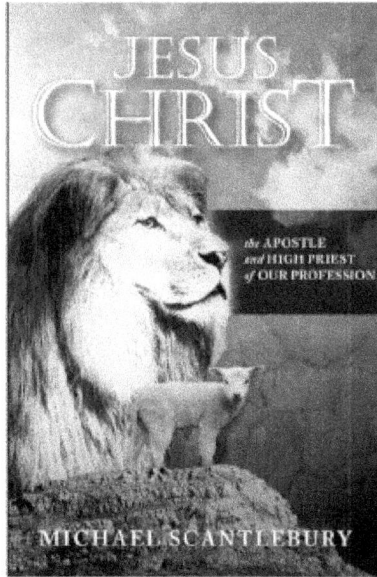

Jesus Christ The Apostle And High Priest Of Our Profession

There is a dimension to the apostolic nature of Jesus Christ that I would like to capture in His one-on-one encounters with several people during the time He walked the face of the earth and functioned as Apostle. In this book we will explore several significant encounters that Jesus Christ had with different people where valuable principles and insight can be gleaned. They are designed to change your life.

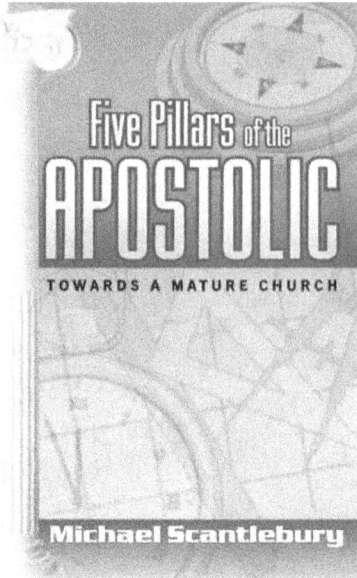

Five Pillars Of The Apostolic

It has become very evident that a new day has dawned in the earth, as the Lord restores the foundational ministry of the Apostle back to His Church. This book will give you a clear and concise understanding of what the Holy Spirit is doing in The Church today.

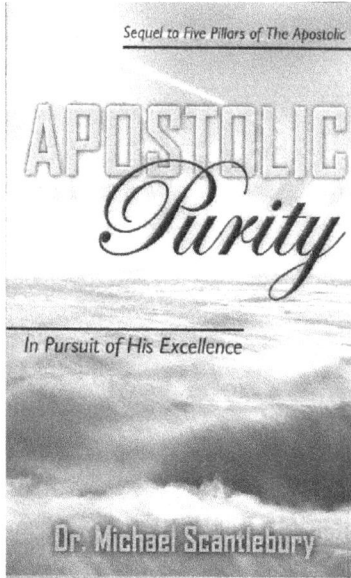

Apostolic Purity

In every dispensation, in every move of God's Holy Spirit to bring restoration and reformation to His Church, righteousness, holiness and purity has always been of utmost importance to the Lord. This book will challenge your to walk pure as you seek to fulfil God's Will for your life and ministry.

GOD'S

NATURE

EXPRESSED
THROUGH HIS

NAMES

MICHAEL SCANTLEBURY

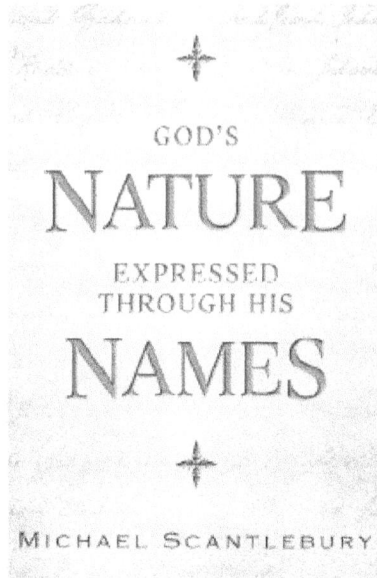

God's Nature Expressed Through His Names

How awesome it would be when we encounter God's Nature through the varied expressions of His Names. His Names give us reference and guidance as to how He works towards and in us as His people—and by extension to society! As a matter of fact it adds a whole new meaning to how you draw near to Him; and by this you can now begin to know His Ways because you have come into relationship with His Nature.

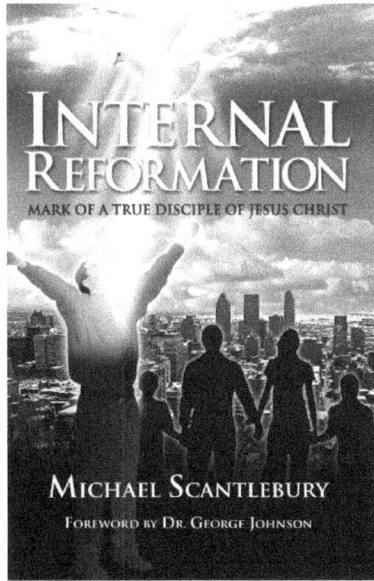

Internal Reformation

Internal Reformation is multifaceted. It is an ecclesiology laying out the blue print of The Church Jesus Christ is building in today's world. At the same time it is a manual laying out the modus operandi of how Believers are called to function as dynamic, militant over-comers who are powerful because they carry internally the very character and DNA of Jesus Christ.

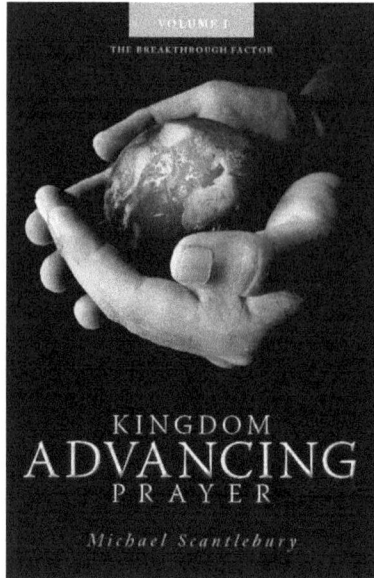

Kingdom Advancing Prayer Volume I

The Church of Jesus Christ is stronger and much more determined and equipped than she has ever been, and strong, aggressive, powerful, Spirit-Filled, Kingdom-centred prayers are being lifted in every nation in the earth. This kind of prayer is released from the heart of Father God into the hearts of His people, as we seek for His Glory to cover the earth as the waters cover the sea.

Apostolic Reformation

"If the axe is dull, And one does not sharpen the edge, Then he must use more strength; But wisdom brings success." (Ecclesiastes 10:10) For centuries The Church of Jesus Christ has been using quite a bit of strength while working with a dull axe (sword, Word of God, revelation), in trying to get the job done. This has been largely due to the fact that she has been functioning without Apostles, the ones who have been graced and anointed by the Lord, with the ability to sharpen.

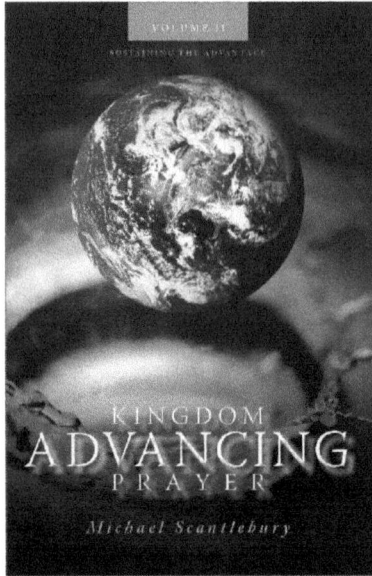

Kingdom Advancing Prayer Volume II

Prayer is calling for the Bridegroom's return, and for the Bride to be made ready. Prayers are storming the heavens and binding the "strong men" declaring and decreeing God's Kingdom rule in every jurisdiction. This is what we call Kingdom Advancing Prayer. What a *Glorious Day* to be *Alive* and to be in the *Will* and *Plan of Father God*! *Hallelujah*!

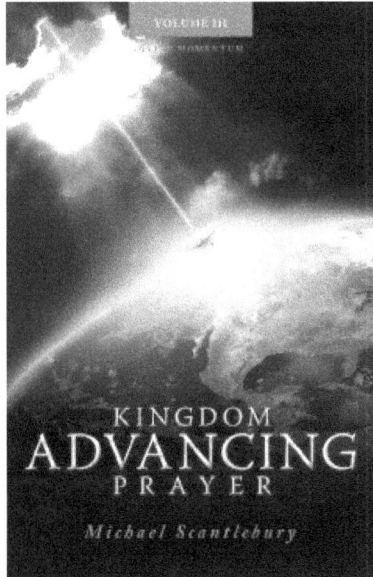

Kingdom Advancing Prayer Volume III

One of the keys to the amazing rise to greater functionality of The Church is the clear understanding of what we call Kingdom Advancing Prayer. This kind of prayer reaches into the very core of the demonic stronghold and destroys demonic kings and princes and establishes the Kingdom and Purpose of the Lord. This is the kind of prayer that Jesus Christ engaged in, to bring to pass the will of His Father while He was upon planet earth.

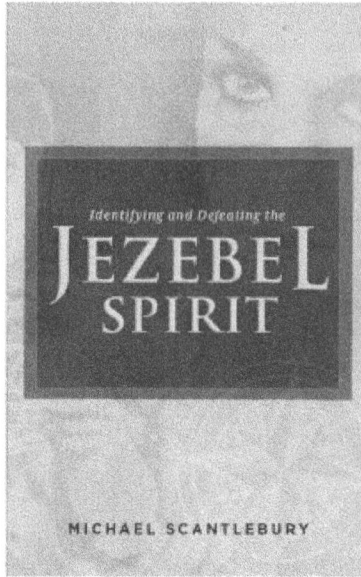

Identifying And Defeating The Jezebel Spirit

I declare to you with the greatest of conviction that we are living in the days when Malachi 4:5-6 is being fulfilled. Elijah in his day had to confront and deal with a false spiritual order and government that was established and set up by an evil woman called Jezebel and her spineless husband called Ahab. This spirit is still active in the earth and in The Church; however the Lord is restoring His holy Apostles and Prophets to identify and destroy this spirit as recorded in Revelation 2:18-23.

BOOK ORDERS PLEASE CONTACT:

WORD ALIVE PRESS

In Canada | USA:
Phone: 866.967.3782 | Fax: 800.352.9272
International: Phone: 204.667.1400 | Fax: 204.669.0947
Website – www.wordalive.ca

ALSO AVAILABLE FROM:

www.amazon.ca/com
www.chapters.Indigo.ca
www.barnesandnoble.com

www.ingramcontent.com/pod-product-compliance
Lightning Source LLC
Chambersburg PA
CBHW061720020426
42331CB00006B/1009